WILLIAM TYNDALE

Bible Translator and Martyr

Bruce and Becky Durost Fish

BARBOUR
PUBLISHING, INC.
Uhrichsville, Ohio

Other books in the "Heroes of the Faith" series:

Brother Andrew
Gladys Aylward
William and Catherine Booth
John Bunyan
William Carey
Amy Carmichael
George Washington Carver
Fanny Crosby
Frederick Douglass
Jonathan Edwards
Jim Elliot
Charles Finney
Billy Graham
C. S. Lewis
Eric Liddell
David Livingstone

Martin Luther
D. L. Moody
Samuel Morris
George Müller
Watchman Nee
John Newton
Florence Nightingale
Mary Slessor
Charles Spurgeon
Hudson Taylor
Corrie ten Boom
Mother Teresa
Sojourner Truth
John Wesley
George Whitefield

©2000 by Barbour Publishing, Inc.

ISBN 1-57748-738-9

Published by Barbour Publishing, Inc., P.O. Box 719, Uhrichsville, OH 44683
http://www.barbourbooks.com

Cover illustration © Dick Bobnick.

 Member of the
Evangelical Christian
Publishers Association

Printed in the United States of America.

WILLIAM TYNDALE

introduction

H e still dreamed of the kidnaping sometimes, when the tasks he had set for himself or the relentless questioning of those who had imprisoned him left his sleep broken with doubts and fatigue.

The dream always began with the smiling face of a man. He spoke perfect Latin and kept repeating the words, "And you thought I wasn't dangerous."

Once again William Tyndale tried to explain how he had been deceived.

He thought he had learned how to protect himself from the most threatening aspects of life in early sixteenth-century Europe. The lessons had not come all at once but had grown slowly, almost imperceptibly, over the many years since leaving England. Tyndale had crossed the North Sea to Europe in search of the right place to translate the Bible into English. After time spent in Cologne,

Hamburg, Antwerp, Wittenberg, and many other places, he had learned to move on before those who wanted his work stopped could find him and arrange for his capture.

Perhaps he had become too comfortable this last time after spending nearly a year in Antwerp. Perhaps he was too sure that the civic leaders of the town could provide all the warning that was needed about the movements of the Roman Catholic authorities in Brussels and Louvain.

Certainly, what had happened was not their fault. The mistake had been his, and it had begun the day he had been introduced to Henry Phillips.

Phillips was handsome, wealthy, well dressed—the very picture of an English gentleman. The moment the young man had first spoken, Tyndale knew he was Oxford educated because his English was shaped by the same Oxford accent that Tyndale had picked up during his years as a student there.

It quickly became apparent that Phillips was someone who wanted to discuss ideas. Ideas about Bible translation, theology, and rediscovering the spiritual passion of the early followers of Jesus Christ. He spoke Latin like a scholar and could read the Greek New Testament of Erasmus without consulting a grammar or a dictionary. He was familiar with the Severn River valley where Tyndale had grown up because his family had extensive land holdings just south of Bristol. He was entertaining, he felt familiar, and his commitment to Lutheran ideas seemed sincere. William Tyndale soon found himself telling the man everything about his work on the English Bible.

When the nightmares disturbed his sleep, they always

began with the face of Henry Phillips.

William Tyndale's chin snapped up from its position against his chest. His eyes tried to focus on the large table in front of him. The neatly arranged books were the first things he recognized. Next he felt the gentle impression of the quill pen against his fingers as his hand rested on the table top. The nightmare faded, and the words on the paper in front of him became clear:

> *I believe, right worshipful, that you are not unaware of what may have been determined concerning me. Wherefore I beg your lordship, and that by the Lord Jesus, that if I am to remain here through the winter, you will request the commissary to have the kindness to send me. . . .*[1]

He remembered now. Before sleep had taken him and the nightmare had begun, he had been writing a letter. He glanced down at his fingertips. They were black with ink stains. Writing, yes, he had done a great deal of writing over the last few months.

He had answered all the questions put to him by Pierre Dufief, the chief prosecutor for the religious courts in this part of the Holy Roman Empire, and he had answered questions from many others as well. He hoped to prove to them that giving the common people of England a Bible they could actually read for themselves was not a threat to anyone. Certainly not to people who spoke French and Latin but could understand only a few words of English. He understood that there were larger issues involved, but he still hoped to be released. If, however, he were not, then certain practical matters had to be addressed.

He dipped the pen and words flowed quickly across the paper:

> . . .*from the goods of mine which he has, a warmer cap; for I suffer greatly from cold in the head, and am afflicted by a perpetual catarrh, which is much increased in this cell; a warmer coat also, for this which I have is very thin; a piece of cloth too, to patch my leggings. My overcoat is worn out; my shirts are also worn out. He has a woollen shirt, if he will be good enough to send it. I have also with him leggings of thicker cloth to put on above; he has also warmer night caps. And I ask to be allowed to have a lamp in the evening; it is indeed wearisome sitting alone in the dark.*[2]

Yes, it was wearisome sitting alone in the dark, almost as wearisome as confronting the darkness of ignorance, fear, and religious corruption alone.

He laid down the pen and massaged his ink-stained hand.

The last rays of the setting sun were creating odd shadows as they disappeared behind the tree line visible through the small window in his cell. Sometimes, especially at sunset, the light here reminded him of other evenings from childhood. But that was a long time ago. Sometimes he felt like those memories belonged to someone else's life, lived in a different world.

He turned his head slowly from side to side, hunched up his shoulders, and tried to work some of the stiffness out of his back. He took a deep breath, then let it out and reminded himself to keep his mind on the task at hand. Night was coming, and there would be no more time to work when it arrived.

William Tyndale picked up the pen, dipped it in the ink, and began to write again.

one

William Tyndale was born in brutal times. Religion and politics had combined to produce centuries of war and persecution, and there was no end in sight. One of those conflicts, the Wars of the Roses, probably was responsible for the Tyndale family settling in Gloucestershire. They appeared in this area in southwestern England sometime during the last half of the 1400s.

The Wars of the Roses (1455–85) was a series of civil wars between the mighty Lancaster and York families who were fighting for the British throne. Lasting over thirty years, the wars got their name from the symbols the two sides supposedly used—a white rose for the House of York and a red rose for the House of Lancaster.

The battles were bloody, and neither side showed much mercy to its enemies. When one side seemed to be gaining the upper hand, the aristocracy and many members of the gentry had no escape. They and their loyalties were well known. Many commoners, however, would move and change their family names so that they wouldn't be imprisoned or executed for being loyal to the wrong house. The Tyndale family did the same thing. When they moved to Gloucestershire, they changed their name to Hutchins or Hytchyns.

By the time William Tyndale, or William Hytchyns as he was then known, was born, relative peace had returned to England. The Wars of the Roses had ended in 1485 when Henry Tudor, a member of the House of Lancaster, was crowned King Henry VII. The next year, he married Elizabeth of York, the daughter of the late King Edward IV. By uniting the warring families through this marriage, major conflicts ended temporarily, but people worried that war might break out again at any time. This was one reason the Tyndale family kept the name Hytchyns for at least another thirty years.

William Tyndale's childhood was probably marked by moderate prosperity and as much security as most people in his day could expect. Disease was always a threat, and conditions were far from sanitary. Manure covered the streets and paths, mixing with refuse thrown out from nearby houses. The combination attracted insects and rodents and left a terrible stench. Most people suspected that baths were unhealthy, and they rarely changed their bedding or the rushes that covered their floors. On the positive side, England had recovered nearly all the population it lost when between one-third and one-half of its people died from the plague in the 1300s.

Not a lot is known about William Tyndale's immediate family. Based on college records, most people believe he was born about 1494. Many scholars believe that his father was a yeoman farmer. In the highly stratified social system of England, that would have placed the family just below the gentry. Tyndale's father would have owned his own small farm and made a comfortable living, doing much better than most of the people living around him. From records of the time, it's believed that Tyndale had at least two brothers, Edward and John, and he may well have had a number of other siblings as well. Because of high death rates from childhood diseases and accidents, as well as the intense manual labor involved in providing food, clothing, and shelter at the time, the vast majority of people had large families.

Like everyone else in England, the Tyndales would have eaten a lot of bread and cheese. The primary difference between what people in the various economic classes ate was the quality of the food, not its substance. The cheapest bread was called "Carter's bread." It was made from rye and wheat. The Tyndale family would likely have eaten "ravel" or "yeoman's bread." This was made of whole meal. Only aristocratic families typically ate "marchet," an expensive bread made of white wheat flour.

English families ate plenty of vegetables—usually beans, peas, carrots, and onions. They also enjoyed apples, plums, pears, strawberries, and cherries. Most families kept chickens, pigs, and a cow. On Fridays, they would eat dried fish.

Many Tyndale families lived in the Gloucestershire

area at the time. Records indicate that they were prosperous and influential. They had important business and political contacts in the capital city of London.

William Tyndale's family lived between fifteen and twenty miles north and slightly east of the busy seaport of Bristol. They probably settled near the town of Stinchcombe. Located in the Severn River valley, the area was known for both its agriculture and its commerce. The shallow, wide valley not only produced many crops, but it also was a center for raising sheep, processing wool, and manufacturing cloth. The Severn flowed into the Bristol Channel and from there to the North Atlantic. Trade routes from all over the central part of England and from Wales led down into the valley of the Severn and ended at Bristol. Large merchant ships departed from Bristol for other parts of England, Ireland, the western coasts of Europe, and destinations even farther south.

People who were not attracted to Bristol by its commerce, often came because of it proximity to Bath. Located about fifteen miles southeast of the seaport, this resort town had been famous since Roman times for its mineral hot springs. In Tyndale's day, it was a popular gathering place for those with wealth and leisure time, as well as for those just looking to restore their health.

It is likely that young William had a very good education. A grammar school for boys had been established at nearby Wotton-under-Edge by Lady Berkley in 1384. It was just the sort of place where a bright boy from a good family could get the instruction needed to prepare him for more advanced studies at one of the only two universities in England—Oxford or Cambridge. If he also had a gift for languages, which Tyndale probably demonstrated quite early, those lessons would have been reinforced with enthusiastic support from his schoolmaster.

Grammar schools placed great emphasis on teaching Latin. Boys were expected to write both Latin verse and prose as well as to be able to stand up and translate Latin works into English. This focus was essential because any professional career—priest, diplomat, lawyer, civil servant, physician, accountant, or town clerk—involved daily interaction with Latin documents. Teachers expected students to show respectful behavior and attention to studies. If students broke rules or failed to learn their lessons, they were often flogged.

School was not the only activity to occupy young William's time. Doubtless, he would have been given regular chores on the family farm. He also would have accompanied his family to the public market. There he would frequently have witnessed criminals being punished.

English punishment at the time was both very public and very physical. The most common crimes were variations on theft and robbery. They accounted for between two-thirds and three-fourths of all appearances in court. If a person were found guilty of stealing goods worth more than a shilling, he or she was hanged. Hanging was also the usual penalty for murder.

Those who stole goods worth less than a shilling were sometimes whipped, usually by being tied to a whipping post and beaten. Other times, they were led through town by a cart. As they walked, they were beaten until their shirt fell off. Gossips and scolds (usually women) were punished with a brank. This device fastened over the head and pressed down the tongue of the offender with a sharp iron plate. One of the town's officials would lead the person through town, using a chain. Crowds would gather and jeer.

The most common instrument of punishment was the pillory. These devices held the head and arms of the offender and are often mistakenly called stocks. They were almost always used during public market so that the greatest number of people could see who was being punished. Petty thieves, bakers who sold underweight bread, butchers who sold bad meat, adulterers, libelers, and people who sold cheap metal as gold often ended up in the pillory.

Stocks held only the prisoner's feet. They were used for small offenses such as drunkenness. Sometimes, rather than being a punishment, stocks were used when a prisoner was captured simply to keep the accused from running away before the trial.

But public events didn't always focus on the grim side of life. Because of its proximity to Bristol and the trade routes, Gloucestershire had many fairs and other festive occasions. The Twelve Days of Christmas were the merriest time of year. Games, costume parties, music, and plays such as *St. George and the Dragon* filled many hours not spent in church services. One man from the area served as the Lord of Misrule. His job was to arrange and oversee all the goings on.

Some of these events were organized by local trade guilds. Every trade group—such as weavers, cobblers, and blacksmiths—had its own guild, an organization that combined the functions of a trade union, a club, and a religious society. Particularly during the seventh and eighth weeks after Easter, each trade guild would put on a mystery play that was part of a cycle of plays. With all the guilds in an area, people could watch a complete cycle of mystery plays. These mystery plays, such as *Abraham and Isaac,* dramatized Old Testament events that foreshadowed the mystery of Christ's redemptive work on the cross. Trade guilds also performed morality plays such as *Everyman.* These plays were allegories that taught about the moral struggles Christians face. Both the mystery and morality plays were hugely popular. Performing in such a play was one of the primary ways uneducated laypeople could participate directly in celebrating their faith.

Games were popular year-round. Children played variations of tag, blindman's bluff, marbles, and hopscotch. Running games also drew a crowd. Follow-the-leader and relay tag had been around for years. Adults would join the children in games like pickaback relay. In this game, players divided into equal teams. The lightest member of each team—usually the youngest child—became the "burden," who would ride on the back of his or her teammates throughout the race. At the signal, each team's first runner, carrying the burden, would run from the starting line to the turnaround line and back to the starting line. Then the next person in line would take up the burden and complete the course. If the burden ever touched the ground, the team had to start all over again. The first team to have all members except the burden complete the course won.

People also loved to sing and dance, and both church music and ballads were often heard. Most musical instruments belonged only to the wealthy families, but flutes were more common among the growing middle class.

The same shipping contacts that supported commerce and leisure also brought in news and ideas from all over Europe. Because of trade, unlike other rural areas of England, the Severn valley contained a wealth of information about both England and the wider world. Seamen were abuzz with speculation about the New World that had been discovered by Columbus in 1492. By 1500, other explorers had ventured down the coast of what is now called South America and had discovered the Amazon River. The English seaman John Cabot, departing from Bristol, had made his way to Newfoundland and explored the coast of North America from Labrador to Delaware

William Tyndale would have been about eight years old in 1502 when the news of the death of Prince Arthur, the heir to the British throne, arrived. The next year brought news of Queen Elizabeth of York's death. Her marriage to King Henry VII had helped bring the temporary end to the Wars of the Roses. The hopes of the British people now rested squarely on Prince Henry, the younger brother of Prince Arthur. Until he successfully took over the throne whenever his father died, no one would really be convinced that the series of civil wars was over.

News and ideas might be discussed in English, Latin, Welsh, French, German, or even Spanish. William Tyndale became the master of seven languages besides English, and given the variety of people who passed through his childhood home, it is reasonable to assume that his interest in languages and his exposure to a multilingual environment began at an early age.

Some of the travelers who passed through the Severn valley were religious pilgrims on their way to any of a number of shrines scattered throughout England and Wales. The pilgrims took their journeys for many different reasons. Some wanted to prove their love for God. Others were seeking healing or some other divine intervention in their lives. Some were repenting of sins they had committed. Others were simply seeking prestige, praise, or excitement.

No matter what the reason for their pilgrimage, they faced many dangers. To begin with, the large crowds that gathered at shrines on saint's days and other special occasions created an ideal environment for passing contagious diseases. Deadly outbreaks of measles, whooping cough, smallpox, pneumonia, and other fatal illnesses were reported.

Also, these seekers were often the targets of unscrupulous people. Thieves saw the lonely pilgrim as an easy mark, so the pilgrims often traveled in groups for greater safety. Vendors sold relics—objects such as wood, cloth, and bone that they claimed had been associated with dead saints or with Jesus Himself. These relics were believed to have miraculous powers and claimed a high price. Many of the shrines were built around what were supposed to be the bones or property of dead saints.

In the case of more recent saints, such as Thomas á Becket, the Archbishop of Canterbury who had been murdered in Canterbury Cathedral in 1170, the claims of which bones rested in a particular shrine were probably true. But the authenticity of the vast majority of the relics was highly suspect and had been the target of critics for centuries.

In the late 1300s, the English writer Geoffrey Chaucer used the idea of a pilgrimage as the frame for *The Canterbury Tales,* a work with which William Tyndale would almost certainly have been familiar. The most evil character in *The Canterbury Tales* is the Pardoner, who in real life would have been able to dispense papal pardons for sins to anyone who contributed money to a specific charitable cause. Among other things, Chaucer's Pardoner carried a pillowcase which he claimed was one of Mary's veils, a piece of the sail from Peter's boat, and a glass of pigs' bones which he claimed were the bones of saints. His most treasured and guarded possession was the wallet in which he kept his money.

Religious leaders had also criticized the reliability of some of the relics and the ways in which they were used. As early as 401, Augustine wrote an essay entitled "Of the Works of Monks." In it he warned monks who were serving God about the ways in which the devil, "our most crafty foe," was working to destroy their good name. Augustine said that the devil had "dispersed on every side so many hypocrites under the garb of monks." These men traveled through the provinces, "hawking about limbs of martyrs, if indeed of martyrs." He criticized these hypocrites for using relics to pry money from unsuspecting people and of living lives that were not true to Christian teachings; then he pointed out that whenever their evil deeds became public, the reputation of all monks was tarnished, as well as the work of God. "Under the general name of monks," Augustine said to the faithful men of God, "your purpose is blasphemed."[1]

Another critic of relics was the Dutch scholar Desiderius Erasmus. One of the leading thinkers in the Reformation that was beginning to take place in Europe, Erasmus was between twenty-five and thirty years older than William Tyndale. He created a famous edition of the Greek New Testament and included notes in the margins of various passages. Beside Jesus' indictment of the scribes and Pharisees in Matthew 23:27, Erasmus wrote: "What would Jerome say could he see the virgin's milk exhibited for money, with as much honour paid to it as to the consecrated body of Christ; the miraculous oil; the portions of the true cross, enough if they were collected to freight a large ship? Here we have the hood of St. Francis, there Our Lady's petticoat or St. Anne's comb, or St. Thomas of Canterbury's shoes; not presented as innocent aids to religion, but as the substance of religion itself."[2]

Growing up in Gloucestershire, William Tyndale would have been exposed to these debates. The area had been a center for religious experimentation for more than one hundred years. In the late 1300s, John Wycliffe pushed for reform within the English church. He questioned the teaching of transubstantiation—that Jesus' body and blood are literally present in the communion elements. He also placed an emphasis on deriving doctrine from Scripture rather than from the traditional teachings of the church. He believed laypeople had a right to direct access to the Word of God. A teacher at Oxford and considered by most to be the greatest English scholar of his time, he devoted great amounts of energy to translating the Bible into English from the Latin Vulgate. He was joined in the work by Nicolas Hereford and John Purvey.

Wycliffe's teachings were perceived as a direct threat to the church, and the church did not want to deal with any more difficulties than it already faced. The plague years before and during Wycliffe's time had decimated the number of priests, forcing the church to ordain men who were not qualified to serve. In many cases, rural priests did not understand the Latin which they read during every service to their parishioners. The political situation both in England and in Europe was unstable. Wars had ravaged the land for more than one hundred years, and the Roman Catholic Church was operating under two popes, each claiming to be the true leader of the church. Church and state acted as one. Wycliffe was prevented from traveling and speaking, and the theological discussions that had raged at Oxford were severely curbed. Wycliffe died in 1384 after a series of paralytic strokes.

Many of his supporters were not so fortunate in the way they met their end. In 1401, parliament passed a law authorizing the burning of heretics. Those who had agreed with Wycliffe's teachings were given a choice between recanting those beliefs or being burned at the stake. Most recanted. Wycliffe himself was declared a heretic, so when William Caxton brought the first printing press to England, Wycliffe's translation of the Bible could not be printed.

Over the next decades, those within the official church and political structure who sympathized with Wycliffe's teachings kept their thoughts to themselves. To make any such public stand would have been a death sentence, but Wycliffe's teachings lived on in rural areas throughout England, including William Tyndale's Gloucestershire.

John Wycliffe's followers were called Lollards. This name is usually attributed to the Middle Dutch *lollaert,* meaning "mumbler," which had also been applied to groups within the European continent who were suspected of combining pious behavior and heretical teachings. Although they had been driven underground during the 1400s, by the turn of the century, the Lollards were beginning to experience a revival.

The Lollards William Tyndale would have known were not as concerned about scholastic fine points as John Wycliffe had been, but they did agree with several teachings that were in marked contrast with official church doctrine. They taught that the Roman Catholic ritual of ordination had no basis in Scripture and that the existing priesthood was not the priesthood that had been set up by Christ. They targeted celibacy among the priests as a cause of lust, and maintained that transubstantiation led people to idolatry because the people would worship the created elements of communion rather than the Lord. They spoke against special prayers for the dead and pilgrimages, and they taught that confession to a priest was not necessary for salvation. In a day when political and church leaders wanted to control the knowledge that laypeople possessed, Lollards passionately advocated everyone's right to have access to the Bible in their own language.

It is not surprising that this kind of environment produced a religious reformer with a passion for languages and a desire to influence the larger world around him with the message of the Gospel. Sometime between 1506 and 1508, William Tyndale was sent to Oxford. There he would take the next steps in his formal education and begin to form a vision that would drive the rest of his life.

two

No one knows for sure when William Tyndale, under the name William Hytchyns, left home for Oxford University, more than fifty miles away to the northeast. Most experts agree that this step in Tyndale's academic career took place in 1506 when he was about twelve years old. While that sounds quite young to twenty-first-century ears, it actually was quite common during the sixteenth century. Often these students first went to a preparatory school where they improved their Latin, among other things. Tyndale probably spent two years at Magdalen Hall while taking such courses. Boys like William Tyndale were sent to Oxford either by their parents or by a wealthy patron who had taken an interest in them.

Life for boys at Magdalen Hall was structured, but it allowed plenty of time for study as well as giving the boys opportunities to take on odd jobs to help pay for food, clothing, and other basic necessities. Although parents or patrons were paying for the boys' educations, little extra money remained for living expenses or the necessary quill pens, ink, paper, and candles. Because of this, most students at both the hall and college were hungry and cold much of the time. They were known for their thread-bare clothing and worn-out shoes, and students begging for money was a common and accepted sight on the streets of Oxford. The majority of students, however, thought these inconveniences were worth the station in life they would gain from an Oxford education.

Classes began at six in the morning and ran until nine o'clock, when the boys ate breakfast. Lessons resumed at 9:45 A.M. and continued until eleven o'clock, when they broke for dinner. The afternoon session ran from 1:00 to 5:00 P.M. Classes were held four or five days a week. Boys frequently enjoyed whole-day or half-day holidays. While young men at Magdalen College were required to speak Latin all the time, the boys at the hall could speak English during their free time.

Many of these students lived with their parents in Oxford. The others stayed in rented rooms. Classes were held nine months out of the year, and young William Tyndale would have returned home to Gloucestershire every summer, where he undoubtedly helped out on the family farm.

Magdalen Hall was a preparatory school for Magdalen College, which already had a prestigious history. By attending Magdalen, Tyndale was becoming part of an impressive tradition. Magdalen was one of many smaller colleges that made up Oxford University. The first evidence of colleges in the town of Oxford comes from the early 1300s, and a university was well established by the end of that century. Many people think Oxford was founded in response to the University of Paris barring English students from attending the school around 1167.

Whatever the cause, Oxford followed the pattern of classes used by the University of Paris and many other European schools during the Middle Ages. It had four areas of emphasis—theology, law, medicine, and the liberal arts. Many of its early teachers, who were also members of the Franciscan order, are well-known to this day. Roger Bacon conducted famous science experiments at Oxford between 1247 and 1257. Later in that century, John Duns Scotus began making a name for himself in Oxford as a Scottish theologian who took issue with the system of theology developed by his contemporary, Thomas Aquinas. One of his students, William of Ockham, soon became a rival in the world of philosophy, and in the middle to late 1300s, John Wycliffe became a teacher at Oxford and earned his doctorate from the university.

Building on that tradition, during the 1400s, Oxford became known throughout Europe as a leading center of religious thought. Its theology department was strengthened when several religious orders, especially the Dominicans and Franciscans, established a presence in the town. It was at that time that both Magdalen Hall and College were founded by a man of remarkable vision and ambition, William of Waynflete, the Bishop of Winchester.

In 1441, Waynflete impressed King Henry VI during a royal visit to Winchester so much that he soon was offered the position of Master of Eton, a new school that the king had founded. Just two years later, Waynflete was in charge of everything that went on at Eton, and he used his position to gain power in both the church and state. He frequently visited the king to let him know about progress at Eton and was invited to the king's wedding. In 1447, King Henry VI recommended to the pope that he make Waynflete the next bishop of Winchester, and nine years later, the king named Waynflete chancellor of England, the second most powerful position in England at that time.

When Waynflete asked Henry for land to found first Magdalen Hall and then Magdalen College, the king quickly complied. Waynflete had grand plans for the building of Magdalen College, but in 1460, shortly after he began these projects, the Wars of the Roses took a turn against King Henry VI. While the bishop was able to retain his position in the church, he lost his influence and with it his ability to use church funds to finance the building of his college. Seven years later, the tide shifted again. Although some buildings were constructed, Waynflete was never able to complete the grand structures he had envisioned.

By 1480, enough work had been done so that Magdalen College could be occupied. Both at Eton and Magdalen, which was named for Mary Magdalene, Waynflete developed a reputation as an educational innovator. He was eager to make use of some of the new approaches to education that were growing out of the Renaissance on the European continent. He introduced the practice of teaching Latin in the English language and of teaching Greek, a language that had been largely ignored in western Europe throughout the Middle Ages.

He also transformed the mechanics of education. In the other colleges that made up Oxford, basic courses were taught by recent graduates who were paid terribly low wages. The quality of teaching was often poor. The Dutch scholar Erasmus, who spent time at both Oxford and Cambridge, described the teachers of England as "shabby and broken down and, in cases, hardly in their senses."[1]

Waynflete organized this system and paid the student-teachers well. Thirty undergraduates (or "Demies"), forty graduates (or "Fellows"), and a number of senior teachers (or "Readers"), in key subjects improved the quality of education tremendously.

When the bishop died in 1486, much of Magdalen College's zeal for Renaissance educational reforms died as well. Twenty years later, when Tyndale probably first arrived at Oxford, English scholarship, especially in the area of Greek and Hebrew studies, was falling behind that offered in other places in Europe. England was slow to recognize the importance of the Greek literature that German, Italian, and other scholars were advocating. Many traditionalists at Oxford fought against including classes on the new knowledge reaching Europe through the Renaissance. They wanted to stick to the courses offered during the Middle Ages and perceived Greek to be dangerous because they thought reading non-Christian philosophers would lead to religious doubt.

Oxford was not particularly open to radical religious ideas that were beginning to circulate on the Continent, such as the need to let common people hear the Bible in their own language. In the years since Wycliffe's translation of the Bible into English from the Latin Vulgate, the religious establishment had never been able to eliminate individualistic religious thinking, but the church's leaders had done their best. The Oxford Convocation of 1408, for example, made it illegal to translate the Bible into English without the permission of a bishop of the English Catholic Church. This did very little to stop the informal circulation of Wycliffe's work and the Lollard ideas that Tyndale would have heard while growing up in Gloucestershire. The law did, however, make it very difficult to undertake the scholarly work that was needed to make an "official" or authorized English translation of the Bible.

Not everyone teaching at Oxford when Tyndale arrived on the scene was a traditionalist, however. John Claymond, for example, had been with Magdalen College since 1487, and in 1507 he was named president of the school. Claymond was friends with a man whose work would leave a huge mark on William Tyndale's life— the Dutch scholar Erasmus. In addition, the influence of Waynflete had not disappeared from life at Magdalen. Tyndale's first exposure to Waynflete's legacy probably took place at Magdalen Hall where the teaching of Latin was not simply a process of rote memorization. It included both the use of English phrases with their Latin equivalents and an exposure to great Latin literature such as the works of Cicero, Horace, and Ovid.

Although Tyndale was gaining educational advantages that most boys his age would never have, he still had frequent contact with common laborers. Magdalen College was growing. While Tyndale attended both the hall and college, construction on the famous Magdalen Tower was completed. This seventeen-year building project resulted in an ornately carved, 144-foot high structure, complete with figures of John the Baptist and Mary Magdalene in the niches of its pinnacles. Final touches were also being placed on the college's original buildings. Carved figures were added to buttresses, and paneling was added to interior walls. Both skilled craftsmen and day laborers put in years of their lives to finish the work.

In the fall of 1508, Tyndale probably moved from Magdalen Hall to Magdalen College and began work toward his bachelor of arts degree. Just as when he had been at the hall, he was not required to purchase books for classes. While John Caxton had brought the printing press to England in 1476, and the first book was printed in Oxford itself just two years later, Oxford University did not yet have a publishing house. A number of short-lived private print shops kept printing alive in Oxford during the 1500s, but the supply of printed books was both unpredictable and expensive. Most books were imported from the Continent.

Because they did not have their own books, students took notes during classes while teachers read to them from important texts. They also spent many hours making copies from books in the library. In those days, books were never checked out from libraries, and the concept of public libraries, freely available to anyone, did not exist. In the library, knowledge of Latin was essential. One hundred years after Tyndale attended Oxford, of the six thousand books in its library, only sixty were written in English.

Tyndale's classes would have followed the same daily schedule as they had at Magdalen Hall. The curriculum included grammar, arithmetic, geometry, astronomy, music theory, rhetoric, logic, and philosophy. As he noted later in his life, theology was not included in the course of study until after students had earned their master's degree.

Hearing Latin and Greek poetry read aloud in class enhanced Tyndale's innate sense of how language works. This was further enhanced by the hours he spent in mandatory church services. From its earliest days, Magdalen College emphasized the importance of music, and its chapel choir is still known for its excellence. Listening every day to Latin words being sung fine-tuned Tyndale's sense of the rhythm and poetic sound of language.

His years at Oxford also increased Tyndale's awareness of the political realities of the world in which he lived. Located less than fifty miles west-northwest of London, Oxford University had many traditional ties with the business, government, and religious power bases in England's capital. In the spring of 1509, when Tyndale was finishing his first year of studies at Magdalen College, King Henry VII died and his eighteen-year-old son became King Henry VIII.

People at Oxford were excited for two reasons. First, because he was the old king's second son, Henry VIII originally had been trained for a career in the church and had received a thorough and wide-ranging education. Sir Thomas More said that he "has more learning than any English monarch ever possessed before him."[2] The intellectuals at Oxford were relieved to have a king who would be sympathetic to their concerns. Second, Henry VIII chose Thomas Wolsey to be his chief advisor. Wolsey had been a master at Magdalen School and probably had also been a student. The university community realized it never hurt to have one of their own be a man of such great influence. The teachers at Oxford who wanted to pursue Renaissance learning came to be pleased for a third reason: Their new king made it clear that he approved of such learning, and the traditionalists could not openly oppose the wishes of their monarch.

By observing and listening, Tyndale was learning that many people in the universities, government, and the church saw change as an opportunity to increase their personal power. Others saw change as a threat to the status quo, and therefore as a move that could endanger their power base.

Clearly, the thirty-four-year-old priest Thomas Wolsey was expanding his power base. While Henry VII had left England more secure and stable than it had been in centuries, Wolsey realized that more experienced rulers in France and Spain could easily exploit England's young monarch. He was determined to keep both Henry VIII and himself securely in power. Six weeks after becoming king, Henry married his brother Arthur's widow, Catherine of Aragon. This solidified relations with Spain. He then took Wolsey's advice and sided with Spain against France. In 1512, the year Tyndale earned his bachelor of arts degree from Magdalen College, Wolsey encouraged Henry to invade France with the idea of helping Pope Julius II and King Ferdinand of Spain, Henry's father-in-law. They wanted to curb France's growing power. Unfortunately, the English forces were no match for the French, and promised help from Spain never arrived. The battles in 1512 were disastrous for the English.

Determined to squelch criticism against his role in the fiasco, Thomas Wolsey planned a new attack on France for 1513. England claimed that land in northwestern France was part of England's domain. Henry VIII took troops across the English Channel and managed to win two battles. Meanwhile, James IV of Scotland marched with forty thousand men across the border into England in an effort to help the king of France by requiring English soldiers to be sent to the northern English border. The earl of Surrey, who was loyal to his young English king, defeated James, leaving the Scottish king and twelve thousand Scottish soldiers dead on the field.

Henry was anxious to go home. The two battles had given him the appearance of victory, and winter was approaching. He did not want to spend that cold season in a tent, no matter how lavish the materials used in making it might have been. He also wanted to avoid further attacks on the English borders. So he had Wolsey arrange the peace agreement with France. The ambitious priest convinced Louis XII to marry Henry's sister Mary and give Henry a generous annual pension in exchange for England maintaining neutrality in the European power struggle. Meanwhile, Pope Leo X was so pleased at Henry's efforts on his behalf that he made Wolsey archbishop of York in 1514 and cardinal in 1515. That same year, King Henry VIII made Wolsey chancellor of

England, and Wolsey had reached the apex of political and religious power in England.

Back in Oxford, William Tyndale would have been well aware of these happenings. During the war in France, prices in England skyrocketed. Students already on tight budgets would have had to work harder to put food on the table and keep themselves stocked with paper, pens, and ink. For his part, Tyndale was making progress in his academic career. He graduated from Magdalen College with a bachelor of arts degree in the summer of 1512. The inclusion of that fact in the registers of Oxford is the first written record of Tyndale's life.

That summer, Erasmus was at Cambridge University, working on his Greek New Testament and teaching. He also released a book called *De copia,* which taught students how to make the most complete and precise use of language possible. One exercise in the book gave 150 ways to say "Your letter has delighted me very much." While there is no concrete evidence that Tyndale read *De copia,* he undoubtedly heard about it. The book was wildly popular among the educational establishment and went through 150 editions during the next sixty years. The principles it taught about transforming writings from one language into another were certainly followed by Tyndale in his future translations.

During the year after receiving his bachelor's degree, William Tyndale would have taught undergraduates at Magdalen College, giving the same readings he had only recently been listening to. His lectures would have focused on Aristotelean philosophy.

Then in the fall of 1513, he began working toward a master's degree. This step in his schooling entailed greater expenses. Master's students were required to purchase their own books because they were headed for careers in the church, the government, or in education that would require ready access to scholarly works. He probably covered this added expense with the pay he received for his one year of teaching and for the classes he likely continued to teach during the two years when he was working on his master's degree.

In 1514, while at Oxford, Tyndale was ordained. This gave him the right to preach in English churches, but unlike some of his fellow students, he had no intention of entering a monastic order. On July 2, 1515, William Tyndale was awarded his master's degree. He would have been about twenty-one years old. He probably stayed in Oxford to study theology, an area in which he showed great interest. It was at about this time that his family stopped using the name *Hytchyns* and returned to the family name *Tyndale*.

The next year, Erasmus's edition of the Greek New Testament appeared in print. Erasmus had taught himself Greek and had become as familiar with that language as most scholars of his day were with Latin. Although consumed with passion for books and learning, in his early years, Erasmus also enjoyed parties and women. In 1499, a rich student of his invited him to travel to England. There Erasmus met Thomas More and, through him, the future King Henry VIII. Erasmus also spent time with John Colet, a teacher at Oxford whose lectures about

Christianity were attracting attention.

His experiences in England transformed Erasmus into a serious scholar bent on achieving something that would have lasting benefit for the rest of humanity. When he left England in January 1500, Erasmus had determined that he would study and edit the Greek New Testament, a radical idea in his day. He thought that in this way he would discover the essence of real Christianity. Like many reformers and humanists of this period, Erasmus believed that Christianity had been distorted by centuries of teaching based on inaccurate sources.

The Dutch scholar's goal was to present a Greek text of the complete New Testament, drawn together from many different sources, as well as a Latin translation and his own commentary, also in Latin. The Latin translation would make his work more accessible to the many college graduates who could read Latin but not Greek. It also would point out differences between the original Greek writings and the Latin Vulgate, Jerome's translation of the Old and New Testaments which had been used by the church for more than a thousand years.

Erasmus worked on this project, among others, over the next fourteen years. He spent the last five in England, at King Henry VIII's invitation. Unfortunately, once Erasmus arrived in England in 1509, the king neglected to provide the financial support he had promised in his invitation. Erasmus did, however, have influential friends who used their contacts for his benefit. He spent some of his time in Thomas More's home and also accepted a position as professor of Greek at Cambridge University in 1511.

Once Erasmus left England in the summer of 1514, he made his way to Basel, Switzerland, where he offered the printer Froben the job of printing his Greek New Testament with its Latin translation and notes. Froben accepted the task, but both men understood they were taking risks. To begin with, the manuscript was quite long and would therefore be both time consuming and expensive to print. Because they had no guaranteed customer base, sales might never cover their costs. Further, the church might choose to ban the book because it presumed to improve on the Latin Vulgate. To try to avoid the latter catastrophe, Erasmus dedicated his work to Pope Leo X.

In 1516, the work was published in two volumes: one containing the Greek and Latin New Testaments, and the other containing Erasmus's notes. To both the scholar's and printer's surprise, the first edition of the Greek New Testament sold out in three years. Many people attribute this success to Erasmus's notes, which pointed out the differences between Christianity as portrayed in the New Testament and Christianity as practiced in Europe during the sixteenth century. These notes took on everything from relics to the hypocrisy of priests who took oaths of celibacy but had both mistresses and children. Erasmus attacked both greed and corruption within the church establishment. In commenting on Matthew 11:30, where Jesus invites people to come to Him and accept his light burden and easy yoke, Erasmus wrote:

> *Truly the yoke of Christ would be sweet, and his burden light, if petty human institutions*

*added nothing to what he himself imposed. He
commanded us nothing save love for one
another, and there is nothing so bitter that affection does not soften and sweeten it. Everything
according to nature is easily borne, and nothing
accords better with the nature of man than the
philosophy of Christ, of which the sole end is to
give back to fallen nature its innocence and
integrity. . . . The Church added to it many
things, of which some can be omitted without
prejudice to the faith. . . . What rules, what
superstitions, we have about vestments! . . .
How many fasts are instituted! . . . What shall
we say about vows . . . about the authority of
the pope, the abuse of absolutions and dispensations? . . . Would that men were content to let
Christ rule by the laws of the Gospel, and that
they would no longer seek to strengthen their
obscurant tyranny by human decrees![3]*

Back in Oxford, William Tyndale was riveted by Erasmus's words. He spent years studying both the Greek
New Testament and Erasmus's Latin translation, as well
as the notes. The questions Erasmus raised and the inconsistencies he pointed out matched Tyndale's obser-
vations both while growing up in Gloucestershire and
during his years at Oxford; then, one year after the
Greek New Testament was published, a single action
in what is now Germany created religious controversy
throughout the European continent and England.

At that time, Pope Leo X was raising money for the

building of St. Peter's in Rome by having people sell indulgences. Christians who bought indulgences were promised that this would guarantee them forgiveness of sins and freedom from purgatory. They were also told that they could buy indulgences on behalf of deceased loved ones who might be in purgatory.

A thirty-four-year-old priest in the city of Wittenberg (part of what was then Saxony) objected to the effect these sales were having on the behavior of his parishioners. On October 31, 1517, Martin Luther posted his famous Ninety-five Theses on the church door. These items were presumably intended for debate among theologians and other scholars because they were written in Latin rather than in German. Luther was a loyal member of the Roman Catholic Church and had no intention of starting a new church. He wanted to bring problems within the existing church to the attention of its leaders so that they could make changes. Western Europe had only had one church for more than a thousand years. The idea of creating a new Christian church was inconceivable.

Enterprising printers throughout Europe, however, recognized the money that could be made by printing and selling Luther's work. Soon copies of the theses flooded the Continent. People were in an uproar over the issues Luther raised. His writings further inflamed nationalistic sentiments among those who wanted their nation-states to be ruled by local leaders rather than by religious leaders with ties to Rome.

The church establishment in Rome understood that their control of Europe was being threatened. They persuaded Pope Leo to call Luther to Rome to answer charges of heresy. Martin Luther asked for advice from Frederick the Wise of Saxony, the ruler of the German state in which he lived. On Frederick's advice, Luther requested that the hearing be held locally. A supporter of nationalism himself, Frederick the Wise arranged a meeting to be held in Augsburg during 1518. Conflict between the Roman Catholic Church and Luther deepened during the following years, but Luther was kept safe under the protection of Frederick.

News of these events, as well as copies of Luther's Ninety-five Theses, made their way to England. Tyndale couldn't avoid noticing the similarities between concerns expressed by Erasmus and the issues raised by Luther. Studying Erasmus's New Testament raised questions in his own mind about how the church operated and what Christian faith was about.

According to John Foxe, an English priest who wrote the famous but sometimes unreliable *Acts and Monuments,* also known as the *Book of Martyrs,* in 1559, it was at about this time that William Tyndale left Oxford for Cambridge. Scholars who specialize in Tyndale's life and work agree that this would have been a logical move for the young man to make. Although Erasmus was no longer at Cambridge, his influence on its studies of Greek remained, and in 1518, Richard Croke, one of the era's leading Greek scholars, began teaching Greek at the university.

Cambridge was also a center for discussion about Luther's ideas in a much more open way than was found in Oxford. Not that these beliefs were without critics. In late 1520, copies of Luther's books were burned by

Cambridge officials who opposed them. Tyndale would have been at Cambridge some time between 1517 and 1521 and either seen the book burning first hand or heard about it from others.

The students who may have told Tyndale about the book burning could have included future leaders of the English Reformation, some of whom later died for their beliefs. The list of the men who were at Cambridge during this period includes Miles Coverdale, Hugh Latimer, Thomas Cranmer, Nicholas Ridley, and Thomas Bilney. No evidence exists that these men knew each other while at the university (people did not commonly keep diaries and this type of personal information was rarely recorded), but it may be that they joined together in debates about the religious issues swirling around them.

Tyndale would have learned from and enjoyed such debates, but at heart he was a scholar. He recognized that he needed a quiet place where he could have time to study Erasmus's New Testament in solitude. While Erasmus's notes accurately defined many of the problems Tyndale saw in the church, they did not point to a solution. Through more than fifteen years of rigorous academic training both at Oxford and Cambridge, Tyndale knew he needed to be on firm ground before he proposed any changes to the world at large. He also realized that such a place would also have to include some means for him to make a living.

He found a solution to this situation close to his childhood home. In 1521, he accepted an offer to serve as tutor to the two young sons of Sir John Walsh of Little Sodbury

Manor in Gloucestershire. Because the boys were under
seven years of age, their training would not consume large
hours of Tyndale's day. And the proximity of Little Sodbury Manor to both Bristol and Oxford meant that he
would have easy access to booksellers with works by
Erasmus and other European thinkers. Going back to
Gloucestershire might have seemed a waste of Tyndale's
talents to some of his peers, but to William Tyndale's way
of thinking, the situation was ideal.

three

When Tyndale arrived at Little Sodbury Manor, probably in the summer of 1521, he was about twenty-seven years old. His new position took him into one of the most prestigious homes in all of Gloucestershire. The lord of the manor, Sir John Walsh, was between thirty and thirty-five years old, just a few years older than Tyndale. It's likely that the young tutor got his job in part through his brother Edward Tyndale. Edward knew Sir John Walsh because the older man had handed over his duties as Crown Steward for the nearby Berkeley estate to Edward in 1519. From Edward, if not from other people of influence who had taken an interest in William Tyndale's academic career, Sir John would have heard of the young man from Gloucestershire who had graduated from Oxford as a distinguished scholar in Latin.

It is also possible that Sir John knew of Tyndale much earlier, from the time the two men were growing up. Gloucestershire was small enough that Sir John could have heard of the boy with the great facility for learning foreign languages, who had gone off to Oxford. In any event, William Tyndale made an ideal person to train Sir John's young sons.

While Tyndale's father was a yeoman farmer and owned a small farm, Sir John had inherited a title and owned lands that extended across a wide area of Gloucestershire. Twice, he was High Sheriff of Gloucestershire. In this position, he was the king's eyes and ears and collected taxes for the king from all land owners in the shire. Sir John knew King Henry VIII from his days at court before and immediately after the young king's coronation in 1509. The king did not forget Sir John, and that relationship increased the knight's influence in Gloucestershire.

As did many young lords of his day, John Walsh made a strategic marriage. In his case, he chose Lady Anne Poyntz, the daughter of a neighboring lord who had married a minor member of the royal family and was a high-ranking courtier. While marriages among the nobility were usually made for the families' benefit and did not necessarily involve a romantic attachment, Sir John and Lady Anne appear to have held each other in high regard.

Little Sodbury Manor still stands. From the third-floor attic room where William Tyndale stayed, he could have looked out on the manor's chapel, where he conducted some services, although that was not part of his official duties. Outside the door of his room and up a flight of five stairs, Tyndale would have found a tiny turret room from which he had a breathtaking view of the Severn River valley and the distant hills of Wales.

He probably spent a lot of time in his room, poring over the books that he'd brought with him from Oxford. His duties with the young boys would not have taken many hours each day, and although he was a paid employee, he was treated as a member of the family. Tyndale's room was not as rustic as it might sound. It had a bed, a table, a chair, and a small cupboard for his clothing and other personal belongings. Closets were not built into sixteenth-century homes, so people used wardrobes, chests, and cupboards for storage. The steep, arched ceiling of the room was made from huge timbers taken from ships, a sixteenth-century version of recycling.

The Walshes probably chose the room for their tutor because it gave him a quiet place to study, far away from the noises of the kitchen, servants, and family members. During the winter, he would have sat in his chair close to the stone fireplace for heat. That fireplace and a group of flickering candles would have provided the only light for reading. The stone-framed window would have been shuttered against cold and storms, but summer months brought the advantage of bright light streaming in through his window late into the evenings.

Unlike servants, Tyndale ate meals in the large, impressive great hall with the family. This respectful gesture was due to his education as well as his position as a priest. The great hall, where guests usually stayed while waiting to be greeted by Sir John or Lady Anne, was but one of many impressive rooms in the sprawling manor house. It featured a high, oak-beamed ceiling and oak-paneled walls. A massive fireplace stood at the north wall, opposite the main door to the house. A black-and-white mosaic covered the floor, and the long, heavy oak dining table sat in the middle of the room.

The multi-storied manor house had been enlarged by many additions built during the days of Sir John's father. Its many wings included bedrooms for the family, servants quarters, a large kitchen, extra rooms for guests, and rooms set aside for study, business, and visiting. The grounds featured beautiful gardens, trees, and a small lake.

The manor house was built into the side of a hill. Its exterior walls were primarily made of grey, Cotswold stone, and a stone-tiled roof was designed to protect inhabitants from the strong winds that whipped through the valley and up the hills. The manor house stood in marked contrast to the homes of the peasants, who made up the majority of families in the surrounding villages. Their houses were little more than tent-like structures built from two large, curved pieces of oak with a ridge pole between them. The homes were held together with wattle-and-daub (a mixture of clay, manure, and straw). Few homes had chimneys. They made do with a hole in the roof.

Most people were not wealthy enough to afford glass windows, and their two-room houses had dirt floors covered with straw. They let their pigs live in the house with them, and the family cow would be let in as well during cold winter nights. Such animals were too valuable to risk letting them freeze to death in a sudden winter storm. Few people had chairs, and they made tables from two tree stumps supporting a plank or two. Most homes had only one cooking pot and a few earthenware bowls.

Generation after generation of peasants received no education. As soon as they were able to work, they began helping the rest of their family survive, either by performing household chores or by working for one of the wealthier families or businesses in the area. Daylight ruled their schedule because they couldn't afford wax or tallow for lights. Once the sun went down, activity was limited to whatever could be done by the light of the fire in the fireplace.

Peasants were allotted a strip of land which they could farm for themselves. If weather conditions were good and disease or pests didn't wreak havoc with their crops, they might earn thirty-five shillings from this work, but they needed at least twenty-eight shillings up front to be able to purchase a plough and two oxen to work the land. They also faced the expense of keeping the oxen fed and healthy.

Peasants were obligated to spend most of their time working for the lord of the manor. Their only payment was a free meal and the continued use of their home and garden plot, both of which actually belonged to their lord. They could not even get married without permission from this man who controlled every aspect of their lives. English ploughmen, as the peasants were called, were trapped in poverty, and few were ever able to improve their own or their children's position in the world.

William Tyndale became quite familiar with the lives

of the people in the small homes around Little Sodbury Manor. Not only were they similar to the lives of most of the people with whom he'd grown up, but they also became part of his congregation. For although there is no evidence that Tyndale planned to preach in Gloucestershire, the record shows that he did preach.

Some of Tyndale's preaching took place in the private chapel on the grounds of the manor. Dedicated to St. Adeline, the patron saint of weavers, the little chapel was the site of services for the Walsh family, their guests, and family servants. No other church or chapel in England is named for St. Adeline, but then, no other part of England was so dependent on the cloth trade as Gloucestershire.

Tyndale also developed a public ministry in Bristol, fifteen miles from the manor house. His light work schedule with the two Walsh boys allowed him plenty of time to make the journey by foot most weeks and preach in an open green. Bristol held six thousand people at the time and was one of the five largest cities in England. (The other four were London, York, Coventry, and Norwich.) Like those other cities, Bristol grew up around a castle on a high ridge in the center of town. It also was known for its abbey of St. Augustine and its large, turreted walls that had protected the port city in earlier years.

Like most preachers of his day, Tyndale recited the text of his sermon in Latin and then preached in English. What made his words stand out was his teaching that salvation was a free gift from God, that people are saved through faith rather than works. His outdoor congregation was made up of seamen, merchants, weavers, peasants, and Augustinian friars. The friars were not pleased with

Tyndale's words. If the people actually began believing that salvation was a free gift, what would happen to the whole system of selling relics and indulgences? Would people tolerate paying the taxes imposed on them by the church for use of church lands? Tyndale's teachings threatened many of their sources of income.

Further, the church argued that it played a critical role in providing the moral glue that held the nation together. This argument found particular power because people remembered how close their nation had come to social chaos during major crises such as outbreaks of the plague and the Wars of the Roses. The friars worried that if the church lost its hold on the people of England because of Tyndale's teachings, society would disintegrate.

The friars in Bristol were not the only clergy upset by Tyndale's influence. The second group of clergy disturbed by the young tutor were among the frequent guests at the manor house. Because of their political and social prominence, Sir John and Lady Anne hosted frequent dinners for people of influence. When he was not away, William Tyndale was always included in these events.

Much of the dinner conversation centered on local and court gossip. Poor Queen Catherine had not yet provided King Henry VIII with a male heir. Her first baby had died during a premature birth. Sons had been born in 1511, 1513, and 1514, but all three had died shortly afterward. Then in 1516, the queen gave birth to a healthy baby, but Princess Mary was a girl. The queen had not had a child since, and the king was rumored to have had affairs with other court ladies. Queen Catherine, six years older than the king, was in her late thirties and soon would be unable to have a child. The king's father had worked so hard to bring peace to his nation. Young King Henry was maintaining the peace. But what would happen if the king died without a male heir? England had always been ruled by kings. How could a woman possibly keep the nation from falling back into civil war?

When that topic was exhausted, conversation often turned to Cardinal Wolsey, the second-most powerful man in England. Politically, the cardinal remained very active. When Princess Mary was only two years old, he arranged to have her engaged to the seven-month-old Dauphin of France, heir to the French throne, as part of an alliance with France. The alliance also included the Holy Roman Empire, Spain, and the Vatican, bringing a temporary promise of peace to most of western Europe. Even the cardinal's enemies congratulated him on this accomplishment. But peace is transitory, and by 1522, while Tyndale was at Little Sodbury Manor, Wolsey had advised Henry VIII to join with Charles V, the Holy Roman Emperor, in war against France.

Wolsey was also developing enemies. He often forgot that he was not the king. This dangerous habit was described by Giustiniani, a representative to England from Venice: "On my first arrival in England, the Cardinal used to say to me, 'His Majesty will do so and so.' Subsequently, by degrees, he forgot himself, and commenced saying, 'We shall do so and so.' At present he . . . says, 'I shall do so and so.' "[1] This arrogance did not win Wolsey friends among courtiers with less political power.

Some officials within the English church also hated

the cardinal. He was closing smaller monasteries, seeing them as strongholds of wealth that did no service for either the king or the church. The cardinal understood that priests and monks were not well thought of by most of the general public. A conservative estimate shows that in 1500, the church owned about twenty percent of all the land in England. Monks and priests often lived in wealth while the people who looked to them for spiritual leadership suffered abject poverty. In 1514, the bishop of London in desperation asked Wolsey to keep a church officer accused of murder from undergoing trial before a civil jury, "for assured I am, if my chancellor be tried by any twelve men in London, they be so maliciously set in favor of heretical pravity that they will cast and condemn my clerk though he were as innocent as Abel."[2]

Conversations around the Walshes' dinner table inevitably turned to the religious ideas traveling to England from the Continent. The number of people accused of heresy was rising. In 1521, the bishop of London tried forty-five cases and burned to death five people who were convicted. While Tyndale was a scholar in both Latin and Greek, the older churchmen who joined in these discussions did not have the advantage of Tyndale's education. They did not appreciate a man not yet thirty years old pointing out to them verses of Scripture that contradicted what they were advocating nor did they like him doing it in front of two of the most influential people in the region—Sir John and Lady Anne. Their hosts, however, seemed to enjoy listening to the debates.

At a dinner at another home, which Tyndale did not

attend, these churchmen explained to the Walshes why their young tutor was in error. When they got home, the couple asked Tyndale what he had to say about the opinions they had heard. He responded with Scripture that refuted some of the teachings. Then, according to John Foxe in his *Book of Martyrs,* Lady Anne said, "There was such a doctor, he may dispend [spend] £200 by the year, another one hundred pound, and another three hundred pound, and what think ye, were it reason that we should believe you before them so great, learned and benificed men?"[3]

Such a question was impossible to answer, but it appears to have caused Tyndale to begin translating into English a small book by Erasmus called *Enchiridion militis Christiani,* which roughly translated means *The Christian Warrior's Handbook.* Originally written in Latin and published in 1501, the book is a practical guide for ordinary Christians, demonstrating how to live out Christian principles and fight temptation. It is based primarily on New Testament passages. When he completed his English translation, Tyndale presented it to the Walshes.

Sir John and Lady Anne were impressed with both their tutor's skill in interpreting Erasmus's work and with the words of the book itself. Fewer dinner invitations were extended to the other churchmen, causing even more animosity toward Tyndale.

These churchmen, along with the Franciscan friars in Bristol, came up with a way to deal with the young upstart who was causing them so many problems. Their plans centered on the next visit from John Bell, the bishop's chancellor and an archdeacon. At fairly regular intervals John Bell traveled through the diocese, or the geographical area over which the bishop ruled. He placed judgment on any local disputes about church law that were brought to his attention. Convicted heretics were burned at the stake, and chancellors were required to attend such events in order to make sure that the punishment was carried out correctly.

Tyndale's enemies complained to Bell that the young tutor was guilty of heresy. Not only did they report the parts of Tyndale's teachings which they felt threatened the church, but they also made up things that he had never said. As a result of their complaints, the priests and friars, as well as Tyndale, were warned to attend the next hearing by the chancellor.

Tyndale knew precisely what kind of danger he faced. Stories had filtered down from Coventry, a town about one hundred miles northeast of Bristol, about a woman and six working men being burned at the stake. The incident happened on April 4, 1519, and the people's crime had been teaching their children the Ten Commandments, the Lord's Prayer, and the Apostle's Creed in English. Two years later, opinions in the church about what qualified as heresy had not changed. The case against William Tyndale wouldn't simply determine his future in the church. It might result in his death.

Tyndale prayed as he made his way to the site of the hearing, asking God to give him the strength to be faithful. When he arrived, he discovered that all the priests opposed to him were there as well. He was charged with being "an heretic in sophistry, an heretic in logic, [and] an heretic in his divinity."[4] Whatever the other clergy might have thought of Tyndale's preaching or have accused him of believing, they apparently sat silently through the entire proceeding, as was the custom. The chancellor interrogated the young tutor, and Tyndale responded to the charges by quoting passages from the New Testament.

Chancellor John Bell faced a dilemma. On the one hand, a large number of local clergy wanted William Tyndale taken down. On the other hand, Bell did not want to get into a public argument over the New Testament any more than he wanted to offend either the Walshes or Lady Anne's family, the Poyntzes. They were without question two of the most powerful families in the area. He apparently resolved this difficulty by severely rebuking the young tutor and threatening him. Bell reminded Tyndale that Sir John Walsh could not protect him from the church's wrath. Tyndale himself wrote that "when I came before the chancellor, he threatened me grievously, and reviled me, and rated me as though I had been a dog."[5]

As severe as Bell's words were, in the end he did not exact a punishment, nor did he force Tyndale to make any promises about future conduct. The tutor was free to return to his duties. However, everyone present realized that this trial did not end the matter. Those who had laid such serious charges against William Tyndale were not about to give up in their efforts to remove him from Little Sodbury Manor.

William Tyndale, less than thirty years old, felt very alone. While he had the support of the Walshes, they did not share his academic interests. The clergy in the area with whom he might have discussed serious issues were either ignorant of Latin and Greek or formed the nucleus of his problem. Having been ordained as a priest in the Catholic Church, he had taken a vow of celibacy and therefore wasn't married. Where could he turn to find an understanding ear? Tyndale needed to find someone whom he knew well enough to be able to trust completely. Otherwise, in unburdening his heart, he might say things that could later be used against him by his enemies.

Foxe reported that after the hearing, William Tyndale visited "an old doctor" in the area who had been an advisor to a bishop. The early-twentieth-century biographer J. R. Mozley suggested that this man might have been William Latimer, a friend of Erasmus who had taught at Oxford while Tyndale was a student. By the 1520s, Latimer had retired to his two homes in northeast Gloucestershire. Such a man would have both the academic credentials and the character qualities Tyndale sought in a confidant. He also would be someone Tyndale had known for years.

Whoever the "old doctor" was, he gave Tyndale some strong advice, which John Foxe recorded: "Do you not know that the pope is the very antichrist, which the Scripture speaketh of? But beware what ye say, for if ye shall be perceived to be of that opinion, it will cost you your life."[6]

Both the hearing before the chancellor and the doctor's words clearly confronted William Tyndale with what was at stake. If he were to continue preaching and writing that salvation was by faith alone, in opposition to the teachings of the church, he would likely be burned at the stake. Yet if he remained silent, the uneducated Englishmen with whom he had grown up and tens of thousands like them would never hear the truth.

Over the next several months, Tyndale's external life seemed no different. He continued his work with the Walsh boys and spent hours each day in his attic room, studying books by Erasmus, Luther, and most of all the Greek New Testament. He took many long walks, visiting people, observing the ploughmen and their families at work, and preaching in Bristol.

Internally, however, William Tyndale was reaching a decision that would set the course of his life. The more he studied the Greek New Testament, the more he saw errors both in the Latin Vulgate and in church teaching. Yet the majority of English priests were still poorly educated, in part because of the stresses on the educational and church systems caused in earlier decades by outbreaks of the plague and war, both of which had killed so many teachers and clergy. "I this wise thought in myself," Tyndale wrote in his preface to his later translation of the Pentateuch, "this I suffer because the priests of the country be unlearned, as God it knoweth there are a full ignorant sort which have seen no more Latin than that they read in their portesses and missals which yet many of them can scarcely read."[7]

He was not alone in his poor evaluation of the clergy in England. During the years when Tyndale lived at Little Sodbury Manor, the Archbishop of Canterbury complained of monks who, while reading the church services, were "wholly ignorant of what they read."[8] Thirty years later, when conditions had supposedly improved, Bishop Hooper revealed horrendous conditions among the ministers of Gloucestershire. He charged them with drunkenness, evil living, and abandoning their duties to their congregations. Nine clergy in the area did not know the number of the Ten Commandments; thirty-three did not know where those commandments appeared in the Bible; and 168 could not recite them.[9]

William Tyndale's frustration with the ineptitude of the British clergy and how that failing ultimately betrayed the people who turned to the church for spiritual guidance continued to build. Did no one care for the souls of the English men and women who were dying in ignorance of God's provision for salvation? How could such conditions be allowed to continue unchanged?

At some point in 1523, Tyndale had a conversation with an educated man, most likely at the Walshes' dinner table. The man was defending erroneous teachings of the church and becoming increasingly frustrated by the young tutor's rebuttals, taken directly from the New Testament. Probably he was not used to anyone—particularly someone younger than himself—getting the best of him in a debate. At last the man could stand the discussion no longer. "We were better be without God's law than the pope's," he exclaimed.

Tyndale's months of study, prayer, and contemplation erupted in one passionate reply: "I defy the Pope and all his laws; if God spare my life ere many years, I will cause a boy that driveth the plough, shall know more of the Scripture than thou dost."[10]

Tyndale's life-mission was declared. He would translate the New Testament into English. Such a work would allow everyone to hear the "process, order, and meaning" of the Bible in a language they understood. Two problems remained, however. First, he realized that he could no longer remain at Little Sodbury Manor, given the heated conflict between himself and the local clergy. Not only did it place his life in danger, but it also put the Walshes in an untenable position. Second, the nation's law forbade translating Scripture into English without the permission of an English bishop. Tyndale would have to find such a sponsor to protect him from charges of heresy.

Before he approached Sir John to gain permission to leave his service, Tyndale wanted to have a well-developed plan. He remembered that Erasmus, in one of his books, had praised Cuthert Tunstall, who had been named bishop of London just the year before in 1522. Like Tyndale, Tunstall had attended Oxford, although several years earlier. He had then gone on to Cambridge, known for its open attitude toward the "new learning." The new bishop was friends with William Latimer, who may have been the "old doctor" whom Tyndale had visited after his hearing before the chancellor. Moreover, Cuthert Tunstall had helped Erasmus with the second edition of his Greek New Testament and was a recognized Greek scholar.

Given the bishop's record of working on editions of the New Testament and his scholastic expertise, it would be logical to think that he would be the ideal person for Tyndale to work under. Not only that, but London was the center of British printing and the only place where printing services were always available. As the hub of

British commerce and communication, it made the perfect location for distributing completed English New Testaments throughout the land.

Having made his plans, Tyndale approached Sir John about the possibility of leaving his service. Both Sir John and Lady Anne remained sympathetic to Tyndale's teachings and writings throughout their lives, but the lord of the manor understood the necessity of Tyndale moving on from Gloucestershire. He provided Tyndale with a letter of introduction to Sir Henry Guildford, Master of the Horse and Controller of the Royal Household. Sir Henry and Sir John shared a friendship with the king dating from Henry VIII's coronation in 1509, so it would be natural for Sir John to try to use his influence to ease Tyndale's way at the royal court.

With the blessings of the Walshes, William Tyndale set off for London in the summer of 1523. He was filled with optimism and hope—and he was totally unprepared for the devious politics of the Tudor court.

four

When William Tyndale approached the city of London sometime around the summer of 1523, he saw a city much bigger than Bristol. Tens of thousands of people lived in London, compared to the six thousand residents of the western seaport. While there were many similarities to the port city he knew so well, in London, everything was much larger.

To begin with, the city was surrounded by a high, broad wall, interspersed with turrets and large double gates. Names such as Bishopsgate, Cripplegate, Aldergate, and Newgate identified these entrances and are still attached to the neighborhoods in which they were located.

About two hundred years before Tyndale arrived in London, wooden bridges had been replaced by "Old London Bridge," which was built entirely of stone. It was the only bridge that crossed the Thames River into the city, and it featured a drawbridge. Houses were built along its entire length, hanging at crazy angles out above the water, and only huge timbers that tied both sides of the buildings together saved them from falling off. Most likely, the young priest approached London from the south. If so, he would have crossed the bridge to enter the city, walking down the dark center passage and listening to the shouts of boatmen from the water below.

On the east end of the city stood the Tower of London, originally used to ward off attackers coming up the Thames River from the North Sea, about thirty miles away. When Tyndale arrived, the tower was used to house prisoners, many of them famous historical figures. The methods of torture used to exact confessions and information from the prisoners were infamous.

Just three years before, in 1520, King Henry VIII had built the Chapel of St. Peter Advincula on the site, giving prisoners a place to worship. Many people executed on the tower grounds were buried in the chapel.

The streets of London were in much better shape than they had been before Henry VIII became king. His first act to pave and improve the city depicted the streets as "very foul and full of pits and sloughs, very perilous and noyous, as well for all the king's subjects on horseback as well as on foot and with carriages."[1] The names of the streets were closely associated with the business conducted on them. Grub Street was where the grobes or feathers were added to arrows, many of which were used in Moor Fields, north of the city. There young men were required by law to practice archery, and it was this skill that had helped England win many battles against foreign enemies.

Bread Street, Ironmonger Lane, Milk Street, Poultry Street, and Wood Street are self-explanatory. Even Friday Street had obvious meaning to people living in a Roman Catholic nation. Fish for fast days (which included every Friday) were sold on the street. King Henry may have made significant improvements to London's streets, but simply because of the nature of the business conducted on them and the horses that traveled their lengths, those streets were still quite odorous.

The main streets all led to the Cheap, as the large, outdoor marketplace was called. Homes and gardens of wealthy merchants and traders surrounded the Cheap. As in Bristol, criminals were often punished on market day, when the crowds of people at the Cheap would guarantee more witnesses. This also meant that more people were visibly warned about what happened to lawbreakers.

London's proximity to the sea made it a natural center of commerce, with more activity than Tyndale had witnessed in Bristol. Ships crossed the North Sea from what is now Scandinavia, Russia, Germany, the Netherlands, and Belgium. Sometimes they smuggled in products and books that were officially banned in England. William Tyndale would have felt quite at home interacting with both merchants and seamen.

Of course, one of the major differences between London and Bristol was that London was the capital of England, and therefore its political center. The king held court and called Parliament into session when necessary. Henry VIII's palaces were scattered throughout the city, and he employed thousands of people to maintain these buildings.

London was also the center of religious power in England. While Bristol had Augustinian friars, London had representatives of several religious orders, including the Dominicans, the Franciscans, the Carmelites, and the Austin Friars. One reason they settled in London was to make it easer to contact Cardinal Wolsey and representatives from the pope, all of whom lived in the city. A sign of the importance of the church in London was St. Paul's Cathedral. It was viewed as the greatest cathedral in Europe and featured a wooden steeple that stood nearly five hundred feet high. Outside the cathedral stood St. Paul's Cross, an outdoor pulpit at which important announcements from the church were given. Like the king, religious leaders had opulent palaces throughout the city.

None of these establishments rivaled Hampton Court, the palace built by Cardinal Wolsey. Between his office and his home, the cardinal employed five hundred people, many of whom held high rank. One reason for his lavish home was to impress visiting dignitaries from other nations, but Wolsey also believed that the use of formal ceremony cemented his claim to power. He forced his servants to kneel while waiting on him at the dinner table. Whenever appearing in public or for official functions, Wolsey dressed in the red hat of a cardinal, red gloves, scarlet or crimson taffeta robes, and silver or gilt shoes that were inlaid with precious stones and pearls. He was the first religious leader in England to wear silk, which was imported by ship from China—and incredibly expensive. Typically, he made members of the aristocracy and diplomats ask three different times before they would be allowed to see him.

From his experiences at both Oxford and Gloucestershire, Tyndale was familiar with people using power and wealth to further their own ends, but he had never seen it expressed on such a grand scale. He probably entered London thinking the process of gaining a patron for his work on the New Testament would be fairly straightforward. So the first thing he did was call upon Sir Henry Guildford, presenting both his letter of introduction from Sir John Walsh and an oration of Isocrates, which Tyndale had translated from Greek to English. The latter document demonstrated his impressive skill with the rediscovered ancient language, and Guildford would have appreciated it because he, himself, was a classical scholar who had corresponded with Erasmus.

In his note to the reader at the beginning of his translation of the Pentateuch, Tyndale wrote that he asked Guildford, "to speak unto my lord of London for me, which he also did as he shewed me, and willed me to write an epistle to my lord, and to go to him myself which I also did, and delivered my epistle to a servant of his own, one William Hebilthwayte, a man of mine old acquaintance."[2]

The "lord of London" was the Bishop of London, Cuthbert Tunstall. Hebilthwayte was probably someone Tyndale had met while at Oxford, but a few years had passed since Tyndale had earned his degree there, and many changes could have taken place in Hebilthwayte's life in the interim. Tyndale was likely too trusting of this man with whom he had not spoken in years. His later assessment is that "he gat me no favour in my lord's sight."[3]

Whether maliciously or not, Hebilthwayte failed to

help Tyndale's cause, and the bishop of London told Tyndale that "his house was full, he had more than he could well find."[4] Bishop Tunstall advised the young man to seek work in one of the other religious houses in London.

The bishop's stated reason for not employing Tyndale may have simply been a polite excuse. For one thing, it is likely that word about Tyndale's "trouble-making" had reached Tunstall from Gloucestershire. Also, the political climate in London couldn't have been worse for taking on the controversial task of creating an authorized translation of the Bible into English.

To begin with, all Europe was abuzz with the story of the German priest, Martin Luther. Printed versions of his Ninety-five Theses had been in circulation for six years, but his teachings had gone far beyond simply questioning the practice of indulgences. Luther condemned the pope's claims of authority over spiritual and political events. He preached the priesthood of all believers, not just the ordained. He accepted only two of the seven sacraments of the church as having come from the Bible and therefore being ordained by God: baptism and the Lord's Supper. He openly encouraged the princes of the German states to throw off their bondage to Rome. Some people were afraid that Luther's teachings would lead to civil war.

In 1521, just two years before Tyndale arrived in London, Luther had appeared at the Diet of Worms, a parliament of the Holy Roman Empire held in the city of Worms in what is now southwest Germany. The Holy Roman Emperor, Charles V, faced a demand from Pope Leo X to give legal force to a papal decree that excommunicated Martin Luther from the church. The emperor gave Luther an imperial safe-conduct to appear at Worms. When Luther stood before the diet, a pile of his writings sat on a table in front of him. Charles V asked the controversial priest: "First, whether you have written these books and others appearing under your name, and secondly, will you recant or will you stand by them?"[5]

Luther acknowledged his writings and the next day gave a lengthy answer to the second question. The emperor then asked Luther for a plain answer, "without horns." Luther answered: "Well, then, since His Imperial Majesty wants a plain answer I shall give him a plain answer, without horns and teeth."[6] He went on to say, "Unless I am convinced by the testimonies of the Holy Scriptures or evident reason. . .I am bound by the Scriptures adduced by me, and my conscience has been taken captive by the Word of God, and I am neither able nor willing to recant, since it is neither safe nor right to act against conscience."[7] When the emperor was about to leave, Luther reportedly declared, "I cannot do otherwise. Here I stand. God help me. Amen."[8]

During the next couple weeks, attempts by those working under Charles V to reach an acceptable compromise with Luther failed. He left Worms to return to Wittenberg and was "kidnaped" during his return journey by agents of a German prince. They took him to the castle of Wartburg, both to keep Luther safe and to prevent him from further incensing the emperor. Luther lived there for a year under the assumed name of Junker Georg and kept busy translating Erasmus's Greek New Testament into German. In the process, he standardized the German language, which had previously been spoken in numerous dialects. Within two months of publication, five thousand copies of Luther's German New Testament were sold.

Charles V, meanwhile, signed an edict giving legal force to the pope's excommunication of the troublesome priest. Luther was officially a heretic and could be executed if caught. In 1522, the year before Tyndale arrived in London, Luther returned to Wittenberg because extremist groups were causing chaos by burning images, desecrating churches, and creating general disorder. He wanted to bring such activity to a stop. "I will preach it, teach it, write it," he told a congregation, "but I will constrain no man by force, for faith must come freely, without compulsion."[9]

Luther's words must have sounded strange to people growing increasingly accustomed to a faith that was forced upon them on pain of death. He was rapidly becoming "public enemy number one" to the pope and the church establishment. King Henry VIII of England didn't appreciate Luther's words either. In 1521 he published his *Assertion of the Seven Sacraments against Martin Luther,* which led to Pope Leo naming the king "Defender of the Faith." Not only did Henry oppose Luther's teachings out of loyalty to the church, but he was concerned that the "heretic's" positions could lead to instability within the borders of his lands. With the popularity of Luther's German New Testament (which went on to sell more than 250,000 copies over the next fourteen years), it was not the time for a London bishop such as Tunstall to be advocating an English translation of the Bible.

This was especially true because relations between the

king and Parliament were strained, and many people felt the stability of England was already being threatened. In April 1523, just a couple months before Tyndale's arrival in London, Cardinal Wolsey had called Parliament into session and demanded more money to pay for the latest war against France. This came on the heels of a "voluntary loan" of 350,000 pounds assessed against the nobility the year before. What Wolsey called "a marvellous obstinate silence" from Parliament greeted his call for an "Amicable Loan" of 800,000 pounds. This amounted to one-sixth of everyone's income. The nobility and the merchants were united in their anger toward Wolsey and the king. The king pretended he knew nothing of the "Amicable Loan," and Parliament in essence told Wolsey to look for his money elsewhere.

With the people asserting themselves in this way, the last thing either Wolsey or the king wanted was anything that smacked of Lutheran ideas spreading throughout the land. An English language translation of the Bible might encourage people to draw their own conclusions about the Christian faith rather than follow official church teachings. And independent thinking in the religious arena could easily lead to independent thinking in the area of politics, resulting in a weakening of the king's power.

Having been turned down by Bishop Tunstall, William Tyndale still needed a home base in London. While waiting to hear from the bishop, he had preached a few times on Fleet Street at the Church of St. Dunstan-in-the-West. Among his congregation was a merchant named Humphrey Monmouth. A leading London businessman connected with the cloth trade, Monmouth sympathized with Luther's teachings and was quite taken by the words of William Tyndale. They became acquainted, and when Monmouth learned that Tyndale was waiting to gain a job at one of the religious houses in London, he invited the young priest to live at his home during the interim. Monmouth later wrote, "I took him into my house for half a year, where he lived like a good priest, as me thought. He studied most part of the day and of the night, at his book."[10] The merchant also commented that Tyndale ate and dressed simply, something that probably stood out in a city where most religious officials lived sumptuously.

Monmouth himself had traveled widely through Europe and had even made one trip to the Holy Lands. Before he became sympathetic to Lutheran ideas, he had received papal pardons, a sign of both his wealth and his influence. His connections reached well beyond the city of London, and his last name suggests family ties on the border of Gloucestershire. He was also friends with Thomas Poyntz, who was a relative of Lady Anne Walsh.

While it is not known exactly what Monmouth's house looked like, the typical merchant with his status lived in a three-story building with a seven-foot high cellar. People visiting the house first found themselves in a large entrance hall, off from which were the large kitchen and its adjoining pantries and other storage rooms. They could hear the sounds of servants preparing meals for the members of the house and frequent guests. Young kitchen boys took turns rotating the heavy crank handles of the spit, which held a large joint of meat over the open fire in the huge hearth.

Wealthy merchants such as Monmouth typically had a

large parlor, two or three bedrooms, an office, and perhaps a small chapel in their homes. The parlor, used for entertaining, was built so that it captured as much sunlight as possible, but other rooms in the house were cold and dark. Coal fires warmed interior rooms, and expensive candles provided additional light. To save on the costs of light and heat, family members and guests retired to bed early each evening.

Furniture, although plentiful, was quite basic. The large, roughly made dining table was an improvement over the long board propped up by stumps used in peasants' homes. Monmouth quite likely had the only chair in his house, which would be placed at the head of the table. Everyone else would make do with benches. (From this arrangement came the expression "chairman of the board.") Meals were eaten from plates and cups of English or German pewter, a practice which eventually gave some people lead poisoning from the lead that leached out of the dishes into the food and drink. Forks were not used. Spoons were made from horn, and men used hunting knives to attack the roast. Knives were also used as forks are used today—for stabbing pieces of food that were then brought to the mouth.

Servants were paid low wages and were in plentiful supply for the labor-intensive work required to keep such a relatively modest establishment operating smoothly. While such jobs were difficult, they did provide food and shelter.

During the six months that he lived with Monmouth, Tyndale took Bishop Tunstall's advice and contacted other religious houses. With the political atmosphere in London as tense as it was, no one was interested in sponsoring an English translation of the Bible. William Tyndale couldn't find a bishop to endorse his work, as English law required.

In his note to the reader that accompanied his translation of the Pentateuch, Tyndale said of this time, "And so in London I abode almost a year, and marked the course of the world, and heard our praters, I would say our preachers how they boasted themselves and their high authority, and beheld the pomp of our prelates, and how busied they were as they yet are, to set peace and unity in the world (though it be not possible for them that walk in darkness to continue long in peace, for they cannot but either stumble or dash themselves at one thing or another that shall clean unquiet all together) and saw things whereof I defer to speak at this time and understood at the last not only that there was no room in my lord of London's [Bishop Tunstall's] palace to translate the new testament, but also that there was no place to do it in all England, as experience doth now openly declare."[11]

William Tyndale was obviously getting an education in the ways of the world. While he lived in Little Sodbury Manor, he learned about the political and religious situation in England through dinner-table conversation. To actually observe it first hand, however, was quite a different experience. His comment about "the pomp of our prelates" is obviously a reference to Cardinal Wolsey and those who followed his example. While living in London, Tyndale also could easily observe that Wolsey spent more time handling political affairs—"to set peace and unity in the world"—than he ever did carrying out religious business. It was well known that Wolsey rarely conducted a church service, and on those infrequent occasions when he did lead worship, he called upon bishops and other high-ranking church officials to act as acolytes—a position usually filled by young boys.

It must have been terribly frustrating for a man who had lived amid the abject poverty and ignorance of the English ploughmen and their families to be surrounded by wealthy and powerful church officials who spent most of their waking hours scheming to gain more power and blocking any efforts to meet the spiritual needs of the people of England. To add to his frustration was the knowledge that parts of the Bible had already been translated into German, French, Italian (the common language of Italy, as opposed to Latin), Catalan, Spanish, Portuguese, Czech, and Dutch, and that translations into Danish and Swedish were well in the works. Why was an English translation being left out of this process? The more Tyndale studied Erasmus's Greek New Testament, the greater grew his conviction that the church was wrong about many of its teachings and that the common person needed to be able to hear God's Word in his or her own language.

These beliefs were reinforced by Tyndale's access to Luther's works. Although anything written by Luther had been banned from England by Cardinal Wolsey, the German priest's writings were smuggled in from the European Continent, especially through the Steelyard in London. The name of the place did not come from trade in steel, although that was one of many products traded there. Instead, Steelyard came from the old German word *Stapel-hoff,* which means a general house of trade. Located west of Old London Bridge and north of the Thames, the Steelyard had been a tightly knit center of German merchants and shippers for more than five hundred years. Much of London's merchandise landed at this place, and workers regularly handled shipments of wheat, rye, and other grains, cables, masts, tar, flax, hemp, linen, and wax. In exchange for favors from the London authorities, the German merchants kept Bishopsgate in good repair.

It may well be because of trade in linen that Humphrey Monmouth first came in contact with men from the Steelyard. Involved in the cloth trade himself, he would have needed access to imports from Europe. These business relationships soon led to more personal interaction. Almost all the Germans living in the Steelyard area were sympathetic to Luther and his teachings. In Monmouth, they found a kindred spirit. The English cloth merchant regularly invited his business associates to his home for dinner, and it is certain that these German merchants were included among his guests.

It is likely that through these dinners, Tyndale both improved his fluency in many European languages and became acquainted with the German merchants. Eventually he learned about the Steelyard's smuggling trade. For among the bales of flax, hemp, and linen, German merchants also shipped hundreds of printings of Luther's pamphlets and books, as well as his German translation of the New Testament. In spite of the tight control they held over the Steelyard, the Germans were running a great risk by smuggling Luther's works. Not only could they lose their business or their lives if they were caught, but they could also be convicted if one of the people they sold their illegal goods to was caught and told the authorities where the books had originated.

Those who study the Reformation used to believe that Tyndale got his revolutionary ideas from Martin Luther. Now, however, the consensus is that Tyndale reached his views independently of Luther, and that he saw Luther as a scholar with a similar mission: to call attention to inconsistencies between the Bible and church teachings and to make the Bible available to common people in their own language.

While living with Humphrey Monmouth, Tyndale made use of Luther's German New Testament in his studies. Frustrated in his attempts to find an official patron, Tyndale had decided to go ahead with his mission anyway. He began translating the New Testament into English, understanding full well that if he were caught, he could be executed for breaking the law. Luther's translation became one of many sources Tyndale used when determining the best way to translate difficult passages, and at times he chose a different solution than Luther had reached in his work.

William Tyndale also perceived a growing distance between Martin Luther and Erasmus. While Luther's writings and actions became increasingly confrontational toward the church authorities, Erasmus seemed to be trying to find a middle ground, some compromise that would appease the reformers without alienating the pope and his cardinals. As members of each side hardened their positions and became more extreme in their statements (in July 1520, Martin Luther encouraged his readers to wash their hands in the blood of bishops and cardinals), Erasmus found his own middle ground an increasingly isolated place in which to live. Tyndale the scholar may well have appreciated the reasoned, temperate language Erasmus used, but Tyndale the advocate for the English ploughman had no patience with leaders engaging in seemingly endless debate while the needs of real people were being ignored.

Tyndale also was able to discuss his ideas with scholars of similar leanings. Chief among these men was John Frith, a mathematician from King's College, Cambridge. He and Tyndale spent hours in the Monmouth home, discussing how to bring Tyndale's project to fruition.

One issue that probably received some of their attention was how to get an English Bible printed. To begin with, London had at most five printers, and only two printers, Wynkyn de Worde and Richard Pynson, printed on a full-time basis. The quality of their printing was satisfactory for schoolbooks and manuals, but it didn't come close to the finely bound products with high-quality paper, illustrations, and design turned out on the Continent. Those books were designed to last; England's books were not. And even if the quality of printing in England had been better in the early 1500s, no English printer in his right mind would have printed an English translation of the Bible without official permission from the church. Even asking for such permission would have drawn unwanted attention to his religious beliefs and political sensibilities.

By the spring of 1524, it was clear to Tyndale that he would never get official permission to translate the Bible into English. This meant that any work on an English Bible that he did would put himself and his associates at great risk. Even if he completed such a task, he would have no way to get the manuscript printed and distributed within England. John Foxe reported, "And therefore, finding no place for his purpose within the realm, and having, by God's providence, some aid and provision ministered unto him by Humphrey Mummuth . . . and certain other good men, he took his leave of the realm, and departed into Germany."[12]

While today, traveling from England to Germany seems insignificant, in Tyndale's day, such a move could not be made legally without the king's permission. Controlling the movement of their people was one method rulers used to censor the ideas coming in and out of their countries. Tyndale neither sought nor received such approval. Probably using his connections in the Steelyard, he simply slipped out of England with some money from Humphrey Monmouth and some other men. He had decided to seek out the centers of scholarship where Luther taught so that he could work with more freedom and have more peers with whom to exchange ideas.

Tyndale was not being closely watched by authorities in London, but his requests at all the religious houses to translate the Bible would have been noted. Eventually, someone would notice that he was no longer in London. When that happened, authorities would send agents to the Continent, searching for the missing translator. Knowing that if he were discovered, he could be arrested and taken back to England, one of the first things William Tyndale did upon reaching the German states was change his name.

five

No one knows exactly where Tyndale landed in Europe, but because he was crossing the North Sea, it's likely that he landed in one of the three great trading ports of northeast Europe—Hamburg, Antwerp, or Cologne. All three cities had printers, and Antwerp and Cologne had large English business communities. Although the evidence is not clear, most people agree that William Tyndale first went to Hamburg and soon made his way to Wittenberg, located in the northern lowlands of Germany.

On May 27, 1524, a strange name appears in the copy of the registers of the University of Wittenberg: *Guillelmus Daltici ex Anglia* or *William Daltici of England.* In a common practice of the day, William Tyndale disguised his name by simply reversing the syllables of his last name; *Tyndale* became *Daltin.* A later copyist simply mistook the *n* for *ci*. In this way, Tyndale began one of his major occupations while on the Continent—avoiding detection by English and Roman Catholic agents seeking to arrest him.

The obvious reason for Tyndale traveling to Wittenberg was the presence of Martin Luther at the university. But other reasons existed as well. To begin with, the university was a center of scholarship, complete with a well-equipped library, and Tyndale would have found many peers who shared his religious viewpoints.

Wittenberg (or "city of the white mountain," as it means in German) sits on a bend of the Elbe River where the river turns sharply to the west. The city was in Saxony, which meant it was under the protection of Frederick the Wise, elector of Saxony and one of six electors who chose the Holy Roman Emperor. Charles V needed the support of Frederick, so he wasn't about to send troops storming into Saxony to capture either Martin Luther or the lesser-known William Tyndale.

Over the years, Frederick the Wise had done many things to improve the town of Wittenberg. His massive building program included reconstructing the castle and castle church, adding three public baths, and in 1502, establishing a university. When Tyndale arrived in 1524, the building programs were largely completed, and Wittenberg was becoming a well-known academic center.

As Tyndale worked on his English translation of the New Testament, he was surrounded by people with whom he could discuss translation problems. Though he could feel relatively safe from capture, he would miss regular news from England. Wittenberg was about one hundred miles by river south of Hamburg, so it provided relatively easy transportation to the important port city. That distance, though, did not allow for regular contact with outsiders. In some ways, Wittenberg was rather isolated, a fact that provided both advantages and disadvantages.

Other challenges presented themselves at the university. Because of Luther's excommunication from the Roman Catholic Church, enrollment at the school had dropped precipitously. Fewer than two hundred students enrolled in 1524. That same year, as Tyndale slipped into Europe, Martin Luther stopped wearing priest's robes. Sometimes he wore the gown of a teacher; other times he simply dressed in jacket and pants. While such a change made sense, given his loss of status within the church, it caused tongues to wag—especially when Martin Luther began arranging marriages between ex-nuns from a local convent and ex-priests who followed his teachings.

Increasing unrest among the German peasants and widespread rioting throughout the German states also contributed to challenges at Wittenberg. The uprisings two years earlier that had caused Luther to return to the university were just the initial stages of what led to the Peasants' War. By 1524, most of southern Germany and the area east of the Elbe River were in chaos.

German peasants or serfs had legitimate complaints about how they were treated by their lords. While some rulers, like Frederick the Wise, were fair and considerate, others were notorious for their harsh treatment of the people dependent on them. One notorious example of this was Count Ludwig von Helfenstein, of the town of Weinsberg in what is now southwestern Germany. He let his horses, dogs, and huntsmen run through the peasants' fields, ruining their crops. This left them short on food during the harsh winter months. He also threw a man in prison because the man didn't remove his hat as the count rode by.

Cruel lords were not the only problem the peasants faced. Taxes and other fees imposed by both the lords and the church placed an excessively heavy burden on these poor people. And the peasants felt powerless to change their lot in life.

The situation changed, however, after the release of Martin Luther's translation of the New Testament, along with other pamphlets by him that called for the overthrow of the bishops and of the German princes. Luther's words were taken by some people as granting permission for an uprising. Radical ministers combined Protestant teachings with calls for Utopian societies. In 1524, Otto Brunfels declared that paying tithes to the clergy was contrary to New Testament teachings. Another preacher said that heaven was open to peasants but closed to nobles and the clergy. Thomas Münzer, preacher at Allstedt, called for all possessions to be held in common by everyone. "Any prince, count, or baron who, after being earnestly reminded of this truth, shall be unwilling to accept it, is to be beheaded or hanged," he proclaimed.[1]

Words soon led to actions. Taking the advice of Münzer, on August 24, 1524, Hans Müller organized a small group of peasants into an "Evangelical Brotherhood" sworn to free peasants throughout Germany. Unhappy tenants of both nobles and church officials (who owned large amounts of land throughout the German states) joined the organization. By the end of the year, about thirty thousand peasants in southern Germany were in arms, refusing to pay state taxes, church tithes, or feudal dues. They swore that they would achieve freedom or die in the attempt. In March 1525, they formulated the Twelve Articles, listing their grievances and demands, which they sent to Martin Luther, hoping for an endorsement.

Luther responded within a month by printing a pamphlet "Admonition to Peace." He denied claims that his teachings and sermons had led to revolt by the peasants, and instead placed the blame squarely on the clergy and nobles:

> *We have no one on earth to thank for this mischievous rebellion except you, princes and lords, and especially you blind bishops and mad priests and monks, whose hearts are hardened against the Holy Gospel, though you know that it is true and that you cannot refute it. Besides, in your temporal government, you do nothing but flay and rob your subjects, in order that you may lead a life of splendor and pride, until the poor common people can bear it no longer. . . . Well, then, since you are the cause of this wrath of God, it will undoubtedly come upon you, if you do not mend your ways in time. . . . The peasants are mustering, and this must result in the ruin, destruction, and desolation of Germany by cruel murder and bloodshed, unless God shall be moved by our repentance to prevent it.*[2]

Luther also pleaded with the peasants to maintain

the peace rather than resorting to armed conflict, and he recommended that both sides settle their differences through negotiation.

Unfortunately, his words were ignored. Peasants felt betrayed by the very man they thought had told them to revolt. On Good Friday, rebels laid seige to the town of Weinsberg, ruled by the notorious Count Ludwig von Helfenstein. When a delegation of peasants approached the town walls and asked to negotiate, they were slaughtered by the count and his knights. On Easter Sunday, some townspeople helped the rebels break down the walls. They captured the count, his wife, and their knights. Two men forced the wife to watch as her husband and his knights, one by one, were forced to run the gauntlet. As the men raced between two rows of armed rebels, they were struck by pikes and daggers and eventually killed. In a show of mercy, the rebels allowed the count's wife to join a convent.

Similar events were taking place in almost every area of Germany. Peasants destroyed hundreds of castles and monasteries. They demanded ransoms from clergy and nobles. Robbery and plundering became commonplace. When church and political leaders refused to agree to the Twelve Articles, they were often killed. Soon even commoners were not safe from these attacks. Anyone loyal to the Roman Catholic Church was in danger. Anarchy threatened.

In May 1525, Martin Luther published his pamphlet "Against the Robbing and Murdering Hordes of Peasants." Shocked by the actions of the rebelling peasants and fearing that all civil and religious authority in Germany would be overthrown, he set aside his conciliatory words of the previous month:

> *In the former book I did not venture to judge the peasants, since they had offered to be set right and be instructed. . . . But before I look around they, forgetting their offer, betake themselves to violence, and rob and rage and act like mad dogs. . . . I must instruct the rulers how they are to conduct themselves in these circumstances. . . .*
>
> *Any man against whom sedition can be proved is outside the law of God and the Empire, so that the first who can slay him is doing right and well. . . . Therefore let everyone who can, smite, slay, and stab, secretly or openly, remembering that nothing can be more poisonous, hurtful, or devilish than a rebel. It is just when one must kill a mad dog; if you do not strike him he will strike you, and a whole land with you.*[3]

In effect, Luther was telling the political and church leaders that it was their duty to kill the rebels. His words appeared just as the tide in the Peasants' War was turning. What followed would have likely happened anyway—the nobility was not known for charity when putting down rebellious serfs. But because of the timing of Luther's intemperate words, many peasants blamed him for subsequent events.

Several nobles and their troops joined forces to attack the primary rebel force. While both sides numbered about eight thousand, the nobles' troops were highly trained and heavily armed. The first wave of attack killed hundreds of rebels. The nobles' troops followed the rebels into a nearby town where they slaughtered another five thousand people. Three hundred prisoners were released only after their wives agreed to beat to death the two priests of the town who had encouraged the rebellion.

Similar scenes were repeated throughout the land. Villages were burned. The stench of dead flesh became commonplace. As the acts of revenge continued, they became more barbaric. Finally, more temperate princes convinced their peers to exact less severe punishment. "If all the rebels are killed, where shall we get peasants to provide for us?" one noble pointed out.[4]

When it was over, about 130,000 peasants had been killed either in battle or during the acts of vengeance. More than fifty thousand homeless peasants wandered along the highways and lived in the woods. The financial losses of the war left few resources for aiding the hundreds of thousands of widows and orphans.

Both Protestant and Roman Catholic princes increased censorship of publications within their domains. Some leaders who had considered moving to a Lutheran position renewed their loyalty to the Roman Catholic Church. They concluded that the Peasants' War proved that Luther's teachings inevitably led to civil war and anarchy.

Luther himself feared for his life. On June 15, 1525, he wrote, "All is forgotten that God has done for the world through me; now lords, priests, and peasants are all against me, and threaten my death."[5] For years, he rarely risked leaving Wittenberg because he was so unpopular.

It was against this background that William Tyndale worked at the university on his English translation of the New Testament. Because of the stability of life under Frederick the Wise, Saxony—and with it Wittenberg— escaped the worst of the Peasants' War. The anarchy that ruled the surrounding area would have given Tyndale enough of a reason to stay in relative safety at the university. But living just across the river from the chaos that was threatening other German states and being at the same institution as Martin Luther meant Tyndale and everyone else at Wittenberg was well aware of the war.

They probably debated the impact it would have on the Reformation, because no one could escape the implications of a civil war being carried on in the name of Martin Luther and his teachings. What would happen if the German princes withdrew their support from the reformers? Then Luther and his colleagues would be easy targets for their enemies. Simply tightening control of what was printed would cut back or eliminate the primary method they had of spreading their ideas.

In spite of these concerns, Tyndale enjoyed getting to know scholars at the university who matched or exceeded his language skills. Chief among these was Philip Melancthon, a brilliant scholar and theologian who obtained his bachelor's degree when he was fifteen years old and his master's degree two years later. When Frederick appointed him to teach Greek at the university in 1518, Melancthon was only twenty-one years old but had already published a Greek grammar. Many considered him second only to Erasmus in all of Europe in his knowledge of Greek. The young professor was short, frail, and homely, and he walked with a limp. Yet he was so loved at Wittenberg that during the university's better years, five hundred and more students would crowd into his lectures. Even Martin Luther considered himself a student of Melancthon and sat through his classes.

Luther also explained the contrasts in their temperaments: "I have been born to war, and fight with factions and devils; therefore my books are stormy and warlike. I must root out the stumps and stocks, cut away the thorns and hedges, fill up the ditches, and am the rough forester to break a path and make things ready. But Master Philip walks softly and silently, tills and plants, sows and waters with pleasure, as God has gifted him richly."[6]

Temperamentally, Tyndale would probably have felt more comfortable with the quiet scholar Philip Melancthon than with the outspoken, brash Martin Luther. He would also have relished the opportunity to sharpen his understanding of Greek through conversations with the gifted young man.

As weeks turned into months, Tyndale's huge project slowly became a reality. When Luther had translated the New Testament into German, he had consulted nineteen other German translations as he did his work. Tyndale didn't have access to any English translation—not even a handwritten copy of Wycliff's Bible. Instead, he used Erasmus's Greek New Testament, the Latin Vulgate, and probably Luther's German translation.

Not only did he translate the New Testament into English, but William Tyndale also wrote notes to introduce each book and to accompany the text. Some of the notes closely parallel Luther's notes, but at other points there are significant differences. Luther, for example, had problems with some of the epistles. He drew his doctrine largely from the books of Romans and Galatians and considered the other epistles to be slightly lower in importance. James and Jude gave him particular problems.

"Though this epistle were refused in the old time," Luther wrote of the book of James, "I still praise it and think it to be good, because it setteth up no man's doctrine and pushes God's law hard. But my opinion is, yet without expressing it to anyone's disadvantage, *that it is not written by an apostle. Therefore I cannot place him within the rightful main books;* but I do not want to deny to anyone that he place him as he wishes; as a lot of good verses are in there." In another place, Luther referred to James as "an epistle of straw."[7]

He expressed similar doubts about Jude: "Nobody can deny that it is an extract or copy of St Peter's other epistle . . . and contains also verses and stories which are to be found nowhere in Scripture. Although praising it, *it is an unnecessary Epistle to be placed amongst the main books which are laying the foundation of faith.*"[8]

Tyndale took a completely different approach. He refused to question the authority of either book. While acknowledging that James does not explicitly present the plan of salvation, Tyndale wrote,

> *"Me thinketh it ought of right to be taken for holy scripture. . . . For where he saith in the second chapter faith without deeds is dead in itself,*

*he meaneth none other thing than all scripture
doth: how that faith which hath no good deeds
following, is a false faith and none of that faith
justifieth or receiveth forgiveness of sins. For
God promised them only forgiveness of their
sins which turn to God, to keep his laws.
Wherefore they that purpose to continue still in
sin have no part in that promise: but deceive
themselves. . . . For as Paul affirmeth (Rom. 4)
that Abraham was not justified by works afore
God, but by faith only as Genesis beareth
record, so will James that deeds only justified
him before the world, and faith wrought with his
deeds: that is to say, faith wherewith he was
righteous before God in the heart did cause him
to work the will of God outwardly, whereby he
was righteous before the world, and whereby
the world perceived that he believed in God
loved and feared God."*[9]

As for the book of Jude, Tyndale decided, "Though men have and yet do doubt of the author, and though it seem also to be drawn out of the second epistle of St. Peter, and thereto allegeth scripture that is nowhere found, yet seeing the matter is so godly and agreeing to other places of holy scripture, I see not but that it ought to have the authority of holy scripture."[10]

There are also differences between how Luther and Tyndale approached translating particular passages of the Bible. Tyndale expert David Daniell made these two comparisons in his 1994 biography of Tyndale. First he looked at the Sermon on the Mount, recorded in Matthew 5–7. Luther begins the passage with these words:

> *But when he the people saw, ascended he up a mountain, and sat himself, and his disciples stepped to him, and he opened his mouth, taught them, and said, Blessed are, they that spiritually poor are, because the heavenly kingdom is theirs. Blessed are, they that grief carry, because they shall consoled be. . . .*

Compare that treatment to Tyndale's translation:

> *When he saw the people, he went up into a mountain, and when he was set, his disciples came unto him, and he opened his mouth, and taught them saying: Blessed are the poor in spirit: for theirs is the kingdom of heaven. Blessed are they that mourn: for they shall be comforted. . . .*

A similar distinction can be found in how the two men translated Matthew's Christmas story. When the wise men left Bethlehem (Matthew 2:12), Luther wrote, "And God told them in a dream, that they should not again to Herod turn, and they went through another way again into their land." Tyndale chose these words: "And after they were warned in their sleep, that they should not go again to Herod, they returned into their own country another way." As Daniell pointed out, clearly Tyndale did more with his translation than simply change Luther's German into English. He paralleled Luther's work when he agreed with the German scholar and minister, but he often chose different solutions to the translation problems the New Testament presents.[11]

As Luther had standardized German, Tyndale made a major contribution to the development of English prose. The years he had spent from Oxford on, learning the techniques that make excellent translations and being immersed in the rhythms of both language and music, bore fruit in his English translation of the New Testament. Five hundred years later, his translation of John's account of the crucifixion of Jesus remains clear. Notice the everyday language that is used throughout:

And they took Jesus and led him away. And he bare his cross, and went forth into a place called the place of dead men's skulls, which is named in Hebrew, Golgotha. Where they crucified him and two other with him on either side one, and Jesus in the midst. And Pilate wrote his title, and put it on the cross. The writing was, Jesus of Nazareth, king of the Jews. This title read many of the Jews. For the place where Jesus was crucified, was nigh to the city. And it was written in Hebrew, Greek and Latin. Then said the high preists of the Jews to Pilate: write not, king of the Jews: but that he said, I am king of the Jews. Pilate answered: what I have written, that have I written.

Then the soldiers, when they had crucified Jesus, took his garments and made four parts, to every soldier a part, and also his coat. The coat was without seam, wrought upon throughout. And they said one to another. Let us not divide it: but cast lots who shall have it. That the scripture might be fulfilled which saith: They parted my raiment among them, and on my coat did cast lots. And the soldiers did such things indeed.

There stood by the cross of Jesus his mother, and his mother's sister, Mary the wife of Cleophas, and Mary Magdalene. When Jesus saw his mother, and the disciple standing whom he loved, he said unto his mother: woman behold thy son. Then said he to the disciple: behold thy mother. And from that hour the disciple took her for his own.

After that when Jesus perceived that all things were performed: that the scripture might be fulfilled, he said: I thirst. There stood a vessel full of vinegar and put it to his mouth. As soon as Jesus had received of the vinegar, he said: It is finished, and bowed his head, and gave up the ghost. —John 19:16-30.[12]

While Tyndale wrestled with theological and linguistic questions of translation, he never forgot his English ploughman. He wanted his translation to be accurate, but just as importantly, he wanted it to be easily understood by his countrymen who were living without the Word of God.

As the summer of 1525 approached, William Tyndale's translation neared completion. The Peasants' War had ended, making travel outside Wittenberg somewhat safer. Tyndale wanted to get his manuscript to a printer.

He also was tired of being the only Englishman around, for during the time he spent at the university, no other English student was listed in its registers. Nor had he heard much if any news about his homeland.

William Tyndale had benefited greatly from his time at Wittenberg, but the moment had come to move on. He left with the assurance that Martin Luther would continue to keep things lively at the university. On June 27, 1525, shortly before or after Tyndale left, Martin Luther married the ex-nun, Catherine von Bora. Sometime during that summer, Tyndale made his way up the Elbe River to Hamburg, where he had an invitation to live with the Emmerson family. They may have heard of Tyndale through one of the people connected with the Steelyard in London and may have made his acquaintance when he was in Hamburg the year before; but whatever their reason for providing Tyndale with housing, he welcomed a place to stay in the large German port city.

Tyndale sent a letter to England, asking a friend there to forward some money that Tyndale had left with the man the year before. He no doubt also wrote to the merchants in England who had promised to underwrite the cost of his translation when it came time to print. Without their financial support, it would have been impossible for Tyndale to get his New Testament printed, and they probably looked upon their contribution as an investment. Copies of a smuggled English New Testament, though risky, could bring a handsome profit.

Apparently, he was also waiting for an acquaintance who would join him in his work and help him connect with a printer, but for unknown reasons, the expected partner did not appear. Tyndale described the situation with these words:

> While I abode [awaited] a faithful compan-
> ion, which now hath taken another voyage upon
> him, to preach Christ where I supposed he was
> never yet preached. . . , one William Roye, a man
> somewhat crafty when he cometh into new
> acquaintance, and before he be thorough known,
> and namely [especially] when all is spent, came
> unto me and offered his help. As long as he had
> no money, somewhat I could rule him; but as
> soon as he had gotten him money, he became like
> himself again. Nevertheless I suffered all things
> till that was ended, which I could not do alone
> without one both to write, and to help me to com-
> pare the texts together. When that was ended, I
> took my leave, and bade him farewell for our two
> lives, and, as men say, a day longer.[13]

Tyndale faced a problem. The friend he was waiting for had decided God was leading him to a different work. But the translator had reached a point in his own project where it was essential that he have another pair of eyes to help check his manuscript before it went to the printer and to proofread printed pages against his original, handwritten translation.

Because of the nature of his work, Tyndale was look-ing for someone who was well-educated—knowing Latin, English, and possibly some Greek. The only available assistant was William Roye, a young man with whom

Tyndale obviously had problems. William Roye was a friar from a Franciscan monastery in Greenwich, England. Humphrey Monmouth, Tyndale's merchant friend in London, knew many of the brothers from this house, and he may have sent Roye to help Tyndale. Roye was academically qualified for the job, but his temperament presented problems. Tyndale could only control him by keeping him short of money. He was known for being hotheaded and untrustworthy. "His tongue is able not only to make fools stark mad, but also to deceive the wisest, that is at the first sight and acquaintance," Tyndale later wrote.[14]

Whatever the drawbacks of working with William Roye might have been, no one else was available, so Tyndale made the best of a bad situation. After waiting about a month, Tyndale got news from England. A ship arrived in port, carrying money for Tyndale from the merchants in England. He was now ready and able to begin getting his translation printed.

Two problems kept Tyndale from printing his English New Testament in Hamburg. First, although the city had print shops, they were not capable of producing as high-quality a product as could the shops in Cologne and Antwerp. Second, in light of the Peasants' War, Tyndale had to take seriously the risk he ran in getting an English New Testament printed in a city that was largely controlled by Roman Catholics. Tyndale and Roye agreed to leave Hamburg, and some time around August, the two men made their way to Cologne, carrying all of Tyndale's books, manuscripts, and other important papers with them.

In many ways, Cologne was the ideal place for printing

an English translation of the New Testament. The largest
city in all of Germany, Cologne had a bustling seaport
and was populated with merchants and traders. It supported a huge trading business with England and was on
the Rhine River, north of Frankfurt, the home of what
was and still is one of the largest book fairs in the world.
The Peasants' War had affected the region, but by late
summer, the worst of the chaos was over. Even in such a
political climate, printers in Cologne were willing to
print just about anything that they got paid for.

Most experts believe that Tyndale and Roye reached an
agreement with the printer Peter Quentel to publish Tyndale's work. Although a staunch Roman Catholic, Quentel
was old, so he had less fear of the possible consequences
of printing such a work. Many people in Cologne supported Luther and his ideas, and Tyndale was prepared to
pay Quentel good money.

In the 1500s, printers faced long, complicated work.
Usually, they made their own paper from linen rags, a
process that could take days but provided a product that
was much less expensive than using the more durable
calf skin known as vellum. Then pages had to be prepared for printing. Individual letters made from slugs of
metal were selected and placed in a metal frame on the
press. The printer then inked the page by rubbing it with
leather balls that were soaked in ink. Next, he would take
a sheet of paper and place it on top of the type and then
screw the heavy plate of the press down onto the paper.
When the plate was released, the printer lifted the sheet
of paper and hung it up to dry.

The process would be repeated throughout the day. Presses could print as many as eight manuscript pages on a sheet of paper, but the type would have to be arranged so that once the paper was folded and cut, the finished pages would read in the correct order and with the type right side up. Each signature, as these groups of pages were called, was then sewn together, and all the signatures would finally be bound together into one book.

Every day, Tyndale and Roye visited Quentel's print shop to proofread the work. The New Testament would not only have printed English words, it would be a work of art. The first Gospel began with a full-page wood-cut of Matthew dipping his pen into an inkpot held by an angel. Large illuminations—elaborate pictures and designs—began each chapter. The inside margins were full of biblical cross-references and the outside margins featured notes commenting on the text. In many ways, the layout of the New Testament resembled Luther's German New Testament, although it was a much smaller book because it did not include the Latin and Greek text as well.

Things seemed to be going well. Tyndale's dream of a New Testament for the English ploughman was becoming a reality before his eyes. But a suspicious customer soon reminded the two Englishmen of just how vulnerable they were to danger.

six

One of Peter Quentel's customers was bitterly resentful of the reformers. Because of the Peasants' War, which he blamed on Luther and his allies, John Dobneck had been driven out of the city of Frankfurt, where he had served as dean of St. Mary's Church. Having reached Mainz in safety, Dobneck, or John Cochlaeus as he was commonly called, soon found himself in the middle of another popular uprising and fled to Cologne. Even there, he faced danger. For two weeks, the people rebelled against church authorities and controlled the city. Eventually the prince-archbishop regained command, and the city settled back to normal life. Cochlaeus was invited to return to Frankfurt and his position at St. Mary's, but he refused to move back to what he considered to be an ungrateful city.

Cochlaeus had already been in the habit of peppering Europe with pamphlets attacking Martin Luther. The latest unrest only fueled his passion. He hired Peter Quentel to do some printing for him. While at Quentel's shop one day, checking manuscripts that were about to go to press, Cochlaeus overhead a conversation about an English Bible. Curious for more information, he struck up a friendship with some of Quentel's employees, taking them out one evening for drinks. In later years, Cochlaeus himself wrote a third-person account of what happened:

Having thus become more intimate and familiar with the Cologne printers, he heard them sometimes boast confidently in their cups, that, whether the king and cardinal of England would or no, the whole of England would soon be Lutheran. He heard also that two Englishmen were lurking there, learned and skilled in languages and fluent, whom however he never could see, nor speak with. He invited therefore some of the printers to his lodging, and when they were heated with wine, one of them in more private talk revealed to him the secret, by which England was to be brought over to the side of Luther. There were, he said, in the press three thousand copies of the Lutheran New Testament, translated into English, and the work had already advanced as far as the letter K in the order of the sheets [probably somewhere in the Gospel of Mark]; the expenses were being abundantly supplied by English merchants, who,

when the work was printed, were going to con-
vey it secretly into England, and would dissemi-
nate it unbeknown through the whole of the
country, before the king or the cardinal could
discover or prohibit it.

Cochlaeus, though inwardly astonished and
horrified, disguised his feelings under a show of
admiration. But the next day, gloomily weighing
with himself the greatness of the danger, he cast
in mind how he might best checkmate that
abominable plan. He went therefore secretly to
Hermann Rinck, a senator of Cologne and a
knight, who was a friend both to the emperor
and to the king of England, and a counsellor,
and he disclosed to him the whole thing, as he
had heard it by the help of the wine. Rinck, in
order to make the matter certain, sent another
person to make an investigation in the house,
where the work was being printed according to
Cochlaeus' report. Understanding from him that
the thing was even so, and that a great quantity
of paper was lying there, he went to the senate,
and obtained a prohibition on the printers
against proceeding further with the work. The
two English apostates, seizing the printed
sheets, fled up the Rhine by ship to Worms,
where the people was under the full rage of
Lutheranism, in order to complete the work
there by another printer. Rinck however and
Cochlaeus at once wrote letters to the king and
the cardinal and the bishop of Rochester, warning

*them to keep the strictest watch in all the ports
of England, lest that most pernicious merchandise should be imported into the country.[1]*

When Cochlaeus learned what was going on in the
print shop, he realized that he had an opportunity to
strike back at the forces he blamed for the losses in his
life. He told the authorities so that they could take
action. Somehow, after the senate secretly ordered that
Tyndale and Rowe be arrested and their materials seized,
the two Englishmen learned of the plan. In the dead of
night, they hastily grabbed all the completed signatures
they could carry, along with their books and manuscripts, and headed by ship about 125 miles south on the
Rhine River to the city of Worms.

They may have escaped capture for the moment, but
their secret was now widely known. Not only did Henry
VIII and Cardinal Wolsey learn of the New Testament
from Henry's friend in Cologne, but they also received
word from the new English ambassador to Spain. On his
way to his new assignment, Edward Lee heard about
Tyndale's work and sent a message back to London. "I
need not to advertise your grace what infection and danger may ensue hereby, if it be not withstanded," he
wrote, adding later that, "Now sir, as God hath endued
your grace with Christian courage, to set forth the stan-
dard against these Philistines, and to vanquish them, so I
doubt not but that he will assist your grace to prosecute
and perform the same, that is to undertread them, that
they shall not now again lift up their heads, which they
endeavour now by means of English Bibles."[2] The king

of England, Cardinal Wolsey, and other opponents of the English New Testament had been warned. It would not be so easy to smuggle the books in after they had been printed.

But that was not Tyndale's immediate concern. He needed to find a new printer, and he didn't have as much money as he had started out with because of the fees he had paid to Peter Quentel. He also was still stuck with William Roye for an assistant, and it may well have been that Roye's boastfulness had contributed to their discovery by the Roman Catholic authorities in Cologne.

Worms, which had only four years before been the scene of Martin Luther's famous hearing at the Diet, now stood solidly behind the reformers. It welcomed Tyndale and Roye. The two men completed the printing of the New Testament probably early in 1526 with the assistance of printer Peter Schoeffer. Because of their smaller budget and the likelihood that Schoeffer did not have type that matched the work done in Cologne and may have been working with a smaller press, the Worms edition of the New Testament was printed on smaller paper. When bound, it was roughly the size of a hymnbook.

Tyndale's prologue and marginal notes were deleted, the illuminations disappeared from the chapter breaks, and small illuminations were used at the beginning of each book. He did add a three-page epilogue, "To the Reader," in which he explained that he realized there was room for improvement in his translation. He described how he had to translate without access to earlier English translations and that he had faced active opposition to his work. "Moreover," he wrote, "even very necessity and cumbrance (God is record) above strength, which I will not rehearse, lest we should seem to boast ourselves, caused that many things are lacking, which necessarily are required. Count it as a thing not having his full shape, but as it were born afore his time, even as a thing begun rather than finished."[3] He also promised that in the future, if God allowed, he would revise the book, and he concluded with a short list of things he knew needed to be fixed. Following the epilogue were three pages of errata, listing typographical and other errors that were discovered as the book was being printed.

These errors were only one of the factors that made the printing process itself complicated. Redesigning the book into something his budget could support and deciding to leave the prologue and notes until later probably were not easy choices to make. It is likely that no one in the print shop other than Tyndale and Roye read English. Proofreading was critically important because the people setting the type were working with a language they didn't understand. To them, Tyndale's work was incomprehensible.

Adding to the challenges was the lack of a university at Worms. Tyndale did not have as easy an access to the reference works like he had been able to use in Cologne, and some of them may not have been available. Apparently Tyndale and Roye bundled together the sheets from Cologne and sent them out to be distributed in England. Tyndale couldn't bear for any of the printing to be wasted and may have figured that access to any of the New Testament in English was better than nothing.

Only fragments of the Cologne printing and two copies

of the Worms printing survive. The title page is missing, but Tyndale later explained that he did not put his name on the book because he was following Christ's counsel to do "good deeds secretly and to be content with the conscience of well doing."[4]

By early February 1526, copies of the Worms New Testament were being sold openly in England by a minister identified as Master Garrett, curate of All Hallows in Honey Land, London. The way the books were able to travel from Germany to England is a story all in itself. To begin with, drought-like conditions in England had led to a disastrous harvest in 1525. Cardinal Wolsey wanted what grain was available to be conserved, so he forbade farmers from moving their grain out of one county into another. Unwittingly, Wolsey's order created a crisis. Grain could not be shipped into London because it was not in a farming county, so the people of that city almost starved to death. The poor food supply made them more susceptible to the severe illnesses that swept through London that winter. The mayor and aldermen of London feared there might be riots. "Either the people must die from famine," they warned Cardinal Wolsey, "or else they, with a strong hand, will fetch corn [grain] from them that have it."[5]

England had reached yet another peace agreement with France that year, and the cardinal, wanting to calm people's fears in the face of a true emergency, told London's leaders that the king of France felt such affection for England that if all of France had only three bushels of wheat, he would send two of them to England. This was an outright lie. France had no intention of sending food to England, and Wolsey knew he would have to look elsewhere—and quickly—to solve this problem. People might be patient about many situations, but when they were starving to death, they could be counted on to act violently. Public demonstrations were one thing Wolsey wanted to avoid at all costs.

It was at this point that merchants at the Steelyard began importing grain from northern Europe. Soon there was so much wheat pouring into London that it became quite inexpensive, and the people of London were no longer in danger of dying. Health improved. But buried in the holds of ships carrying grain were copies of Tyndale's New Testament. The men of the Steelyard carefully moved their banned cargo through the docks and warehouses to book dealers in London and throughout the rest of the nation.

Smugglers used other methods to get the Testaments in as well. In an article about smuggling books during this time, F. C. Avis described the process this way: "Barrels or casks, apparently full of wine or oil, might secrete watertight boxes holding dangerous propaganda. Cargoes of wheat or grain, hides or skins were not always made up exclusively of these items. Flour sacks often held carefully packed contraband books strategically placed in the meal. Chests with false sides or bases, hidden receptacles or secret compartments brought over documents."[6] Smugglers also secretly marked bales of cloth, inside of which were hidden flat, printed sheets. Once delivered, those sheets would be folded, stitched, cut, and bound into books.

Roman Catholic historian L. A. Schuster described the situation in these words:

> *Already toward the end of March 1526, along the arteries leading to London, through ports and rivers and creeks along the eastern seaboard and across the heaths and marshes of East Anglia the explosive copies of the first printed English New Testament were being smuggled.*
>
> *". . . there comes a power*
> *Into this scatter'd kingdom; who already,*
> *Wise in our negligence, have secret feet*
> *In some of our best ports, and are at point*
> *To show their open banner."*
> *(King Lear, III.i.30–4)*
>
> *The English protestant reformation was entering a radically new phase. Bursting its containment of learned Latin enclaves and clerical outposts, it was carrying the war into the market place and would soon arm the common man with an ageless weapon of religious revolution.*[7]

The Testaments cost about half what a laborer earned in a week. While that represented a lot of money to a poor laborer, it was still within reach. (For a modern comparison, based on the federal minimum wage of $5.15 per hour, a full-time worker earning minimum wage would pay $103 for a New Testament.) Neighbors chipped in together to buy one New Testament. They would find a person who had basic reading skills and gather around to hear for the first time the New Testament read in their own language. Bartering also occurred. A poor man might offer a load of hay in exchange for a New Testament. Soon Tyndale's English ploughman and people of every economic level in the country were hearing the Bible in their own language. It was a revelation, and demand for the banned books grew.

The first copies of the New Testament arrived in London at an ideal time from the smugglers' viewpoint. Cuthbert Tunstall, bishop of London, was out of the country until August, and Cardinal Wolsey and the king were occupied with international affairs. The peace with France was fragile, and during 1526 Europe was threatened by an invasion led by Suleiman the Magnificent, ruler of the Ottoman Empire.

Charles V, the Holy Roman Emperor, was holding King Francis I of France captive. Francis managed to get a letter to Suleiman, asking the Ottoman emperor to attack Hungary to avenge his capture. While Suleiman considered Francis's request, the French king tricked Charles by signing legal documents that promised a number of concessions in exchange for his freedom. What Charles didn't know was that earlier Francis had managed to secretly sign a document that made any future paper he signed while in Charles's custody null and void. The document had been safely smuggled back to France. On the weight of his false promises, Francis managed to return to France, but in the meantime, Suleiman attacked Hungary.

Pope Clement VII asked Christian leaders throughout Europe to go to the aid of Hungary. Lutheran leaders encouraged the German princes not to join in fighting Suleiman because they saw this invasion as God's judgment. To resist Suleiman would be to resist God. The princes took their advice and stayed home. Charles V, the Holy Roman Emperor, was busy sacking Rome and taking the pope captive in return for Clement having sided with Francis when terms for the French king's release had been made public. In the face of weak opposition, Suleiman conquered Hungary with ease.

When Henry VIII learned that this "infidel" had taken over part of Europe simply because the Lutheran German states refused to help in the battle against Suleiman, he had one more reason to dislike Protestant ideas. People who accepted these ideas were willing to let Christian civilization be overrun by Islam rather than follow the advice of the pope.

Henry was distracted by another issue as well. By 1526, it was clear to everyone that Queen Catherine would not have any more children. In those days, a forty-one-year-old woman was usually incapable of having children. This likelihood was greater in Catherine's case because of her many miscarriages and illnesses. People who saw her noted that she looked much older than she was.

Further, although it was not generally known at the time, Henry himself recorded that in 1524 he stopped having marital relations with his wife. Ten years before that, he had contemplated getting his marriage annulled by the pope, but he'd set aside the idea after Catherine had given birth to Princess Mary. Now having given up on ever having a son by Queen Catherine, Henry was quietly considering the best way to end his marriage. He didn't think that Catherine was a bad wife—by all accounts she was cultured, refined, and faithful, and she truly loved her husband. But the king desperately wanted a son to guarantee that when he died, the kingdom could continue without being torn apart by varying parties fighting for the crown.

It was true that Henry VIII had an illegitimate son who was born in 1519. Other monarchs had named such sons as their successors. Although Henry made the boy Duke of Richmond and Somerset, he gradually realized that only a legitimate, direct male heir to the throne would spare his nation from returning to the horrors of the Wars of the Roses. Henry was only the second Tudor king since the end of those wars, and a number of people with family ties to the throne might lay claim to it if they felt they could successfully challenge the claims of Henry's illegitimate son.

Some historians suspect that Henry became enamored with Anne Boleyn at about this time. She had become lady-in-waiting to Queen Catherine four years earlier at the age of fifteen. Although not beautiful, her flashing eyes, flowing dark hair, grace, wit, and love of life charmed many men in the king's court. Letters and other records show that the king was definitely attached to the young woman by 1527, but it is possible that the attraction began the previous year. No other woman lay claim to his affections in 1526, and the king rarely went as long as a year without some love interest.

In spite of these distractions, the presence of English New Testaments in England could not be kept from the authorities forever—especially when clergy such as

Master Garrett of London were openly advertising them. By August, Tunstall had returned to England and gotten his hands on a copy of Tyndale's work. He had even more reasons now to be opposed to an English translation of the Bible than he had had three years earlier when Tyndale had first approached him with the idea. Outraged at what was obviously both a threat to the institutional church and a violation of English law, Tunstall met with other bishops and Cardinal Wolsey to discuss their response.

The results of the meeting were hardly a surprise. Copies of the book would be sought out and destroyed. Watch must be kept at all the ports, and government agents were assigned to search incoming cargo for contraband. Buying, selling, or simply handling the book became a serious offense.

On October 24, 1526, Bishop Tunstall sent a directive to his archdeacons, complaining about the New Testament written in the common tongue, which he identified as the work of William Tyndale and William Roye. The translation was intermingled with "certain articles of heretical depravity and pernicious erroneous opinions, pestilent, scandalous, and seductive of simple minds. . .of which translation many books, containing the pestilent and pernicious poison in the vulgar [common] tongue, have been dispersed in great numbers throughout our diocese; which truly, unless it be speedily foreseen will without doubt infect and contaminate the flock committed to us, with the pestilent poison and the deadly disease of heretical depravity."[8] His words were designed to grab the attention of the most lackadaisical member of the clergy. Within thirty days, he went on to say, all copies of the English

New Testament must be brought in to church authorities or the possessors of these documents would be charged with heresy.

The bishop of London wasn't through. The next day he called in London's booksellers for a private meeting. He bluntly warned them what they were risking if they continued to deal with Lutheran books written in either Latin or English. Some of his eagerness to lay down the law on this issue may have grown from frustration that he was supposed to be bishop of London, but Cardinal Wolsey was constantly taking charge of issues that right-fully belonged to Tunstall.

Two days later, the bishop gave a sermon at St. Paul's Cross, outside the west door of St. Paul's Cathedral and the traditional site of important announcements being made by church officials. He preached against both Tyndale and the English New Testament. He claimed to have found two thousand errors in the book, something which modern scholars cannot duplicate. When Tyndale, back in Europe, heard of the bishop's claim, he wryly remarked that if the bishops found the letter *i* undotted, they would expose it as proof of heresy.

Having completed his sermon, Tunstall created a dramatic image for his listeners to take home with them. He took a copy of Tyndale's New Testament and threw it onto a blazing fire. Book burning had become fairly common in England, but the bishop's action no doubt reminded people of what happened to heretics.

When Tyndale later heard of the bishop's action, he commented, "In burning the New Testament they did none other thing that I looked for; no more shall they do if they burn me also, if it be God's will it shall so be. Nevertheless, in translating the New Testament I did my duty."[9] His words do not fully reveal how shaken he was by the news. Tyndale, and many of his peers, drew a distinction between ordinary books and the Bible. Burning books was one thing, but to burn any part of the Bible—even if it were written in English—shocked them. How could a man of the church destroy the very words of God?

Tyndale was also distressed because he knew the bishop was a Greek scholar and friend of Erasmus. More than just about anyone else, Bishop Tunstall should have understood how closely Tyndale's translation reflected the words and spirit of the Greek New Testament. How could he publicly question what Tyndale had done and in such an exaggerated way?

Tyndale was not alone in his bewilderment. John Lambert, a scholar from Cambridge, recorded his reaction to the bishop's sermon: "Moreover I was at Paul's Cross, when the New Testament, imprinted of late beyond the sea, was first forefended; and truly my heart lamented greatly to hear a great man preaching against it, who showed forth certain things that he noted for hideous errors to be in it, that I, yea and not only I, but likewise did many others, think verily to be none. But (alack for pity!) malice cannot say well. God help us all, and amend it."[10] Lambert and others he spoke with at the time attributed the action to Tunstall's maliciousness.

In spite of Tunstall's efforts to destroy Tyndale's work, the supply of New Testaments in England increased. By November of that same year, a pirated copy of Tyndale's work was flowing into the country. Christopher von

Endhoven of Antwerp, Belgium, printed about three thousand copies of the New Testament. These books were printed on much smaller paper than the Worms edition and had not been well proofread, but because of their size, they were easier to smuggle.

Combined with the printing from Worms, about six thousand English New Testaments were in circulation. This represented a huge number of copies at that time. Most print runs in Europe at the beginning of the sixteenth century numbered between one thousand and fifteen hundred copies. Even Luther's German New Testament had a first print run of just four thousand copies. Assuming the numbers of English New Testaments reported by Tyndale's contemporaries are correct, the translator understood quite well what a demand existed among the people in England for possessing any part of the Bible written in their own language.

Tyndale was not the only person who read the situation correctly. Cardinal Wolsey knew too well what would happen if enough people got their hands on an English New Testament, and he feared the situation was getting out of hand. He sent instructions to Sir John Hackett, English ambassador to the Low Countries, which were received by the ambassador on November 21, 1526. Wolsey ordered Hackett to take action against printers, booksellers, and anyone else in the region who was involved in the production and/or distribution of the English New Testaments. The cardinal thought that cutting off the supply might be the best solution to his problem.

Sir John took his instructions seriously, and by mid-January 1527, he had collected enough copies of the

English New Testament to supply book burnings in Antwerp and Bergen-op-Zoom, a city along the southwestern coast of what is now the Netherlands. He also received letters from Wolsey to deliver to Princess Margaret, the regent of the Low Countries, and to the governor of the English House of Merchants in Antwerp. The eventual result was that Christopher von Endhoven was arrested and, after what seemed an interminable series of delays to Sir John, the printer's books and presses were destroyed.

It wasn't enough. Sir John Hackett soon found himself making constant trips between Antwerp, Frankfurt, Barrow, Zeeland, and other Low Country cities, seizing books and printers. It was in many ways a frustrating experience. Once he reached the harbor of Zeeland only to discover that a shipment of books had left for Scotland the day before. He also was too late in learning that more than two thousand English books—which likely included copies of Tyndale's New Testament—had been offered for sale at the April 1527 book fair in Frankfurt. Hackett had his successes, but the printing and distribution system on the Continent was much too efficient for one English ambassador to be able to stop.

Back in England, even King Henry was weighing in on the matter. "We. . .with the deliberate advice of Thomas Lord Cardinal [Wolsey] and other reverend fathers of the spirituality, have determined the said and untrue translations to be burned," he declared in February 1527, adding, "with further sharp correction and punishment against the keepers and readers of the same."[11]

While the church establishment was united in its

desire to stamp out the English New Testament, they did not share the same degree of business savvy. In May 1527, Archbishop Warham came up with a novel approach to ridding the world of Tyndale's work. He suggested to his bishops that they contribute money for buying up all the copies of the New Testament that were available. Bishop Nix of Norwich sent in his donation along with a letter complimenting his superior on this "gracious and blessed deed" for which God would highly reward him.[12] Apparently neither man considered what would happen to the money they were using to buy the New Testaments. The action ultimately pleased everyone. The bishops had Testaments to burn, the merchants made a profit on the sale, and Tyndale received money from the sales to help finance further printing of his New Testament.

While all this was happening in England, William Tyndale was busy in Worms with his own problems. Chief among these problems was his assistant William Roye. Rarely has an assistant been both so desperately needed and so greatly despised. At least Roye's penchant for talking to strangers about things that were best kept secret did not present as great a threat in solidly Lutheran Worms. Still, Tyndale must have breathed a sigh of relief when the months of printing and proofreading were completed and his New Testaments began to make their way to England. At last the work was done, and he could part ways with Roye. Tyndale's former assistant took up new friends and made some money. Then Roye left for Strasbourg, Germany, about 350 miles to the northwest of Worms.

News of Roye's departure must have pleased Tyndale.

Worms may not have been large enough for both Englishmen's comfort. His relief was short-lived. Before long,
Tyndale began receiving reports of his former assistant
exaggerating his abilities and boasting about his accomplishments. Tyndale knew that Roye was not as good a
scholar as he was leading people to believe.

In May of 1527, at the same time that Sir John Hackett
was roaming Northern Europe, looking for copies of
Tyndale's translation and having people thrown into jail,
Tyndale received a visit from Brother Jerome Barlow. This
man had belonged to the same Franciscan monastery in
Greenwich, England, that Roye had come from. Jerome
was dissatisfied with the way the church was being run.
He intended to join Roye in Strasbourg.

Tyndale warned Jerome of the dangers of working
with William Roye. "Jerome with all diligence I warned
of Roye's boldness and exhorted him to beware of him
and to walk quietly and with all patience," he recorded.[13]
Jerome chose to ignore Tyndale's advice. "Nevertheless
when he was come to Argentine [Strasbourg] William
Roye . . .gat him to him and set him a work to make
rhymes, while he himself translated a dialogue out of
Latin into English, in whose prologue he promiseth
more a great deal than I fear me he will ever pay."[14]

Tyndale would not know for another year what exactly
the two men were writing, but when it was revealed,
that project created more problems for the English
translator. Trouble enough was already descending on
William Tyndale. As an Englishman, he could not expect
the same protection from the German princes who were

sympathetic to reformed ideas that Luther and his German colleagues received. Over the months, he heard reports of the book burnings in England and of Sir John Hackett's work in Europe. He became convinced that staying in Worms put him in too vulnerable a position. With the efforts that were being made to destroy his work, Tyndale surmised that it wouldn't be long before the king's men began seeking to destroy the translator. He decided to move to a more remote location where he would be less likely to be discovered or betrayed.

Probably a short time after Tyndale's meeting with Jerome Barlow, he left Worms for Marburg, about eighty miles northwest of Worms and one hundred miles north of Frankfurt. While Marburg was both small and far away from the areas where English agents were looking for Tyndale's books, it was hardly inconsequential.

Marburg was the capital of the German state of Hesse. As Tyndale approached Marburg, he would have seen a classic medieval city. Built on a hill, it was dominated by the Schloá or castle where the counts of Hessen ruled. Small, twisting streets led up to the castle. At the time, Hesse was ruled by Landgrave Phillip the Magnanimous.

Phillip had converted to Lutheran beliefs in 1524. During the Peasants' War, he joined with Frederick, the elector of Saxony, and various dukes of the area to put down a peasant revolt and is credited with saving the central German states from destruction. His sympathies, however, still remained strongly Lutheran, and he was the first German leader to realize that Protestant towns and rulers would have to unite to protect themselves from the Roman

Catholic princes of the south who were determined to overthrow their Lutheran counterparts. He succeeded in convincing his peers to join with him and began turning Hesse into a Lutheran state.

In 1527, the same year Tyndale arrived in Marburg, Phillip founded the first Protestant university in Europe, Phillips University. Its purpose was to insure that the next generation of clergy and state officials would be educated along Lutheran lines. The school quickly became famous, but at the time Tyndale was in Marburg, it was just beginning. Tyndale would have had the advantage of living in the relative safety of a strongly Lutheran state, having access to reference materials from the young university, and being away from much of the controversy that had hounded him in Cologne and Worms.

His initial plans were to continue his studies and translation work, but events in the wider world were about to intervene. Once again, William Tyndale would be forced to take a more active role than that of a reclusive scholar.

seven

B y the late summer of 1527, thousands of Tyndale's New Testaments had reached England. Many of these books were being gathered to be burned, and Cardinal Wolsey decided it was long past time to put pressure directly on the sellers and owners of these books. One of the first groups he attacked was some scholars at Cambridge. Among them was Thomas Bilney, affectionately called "Little Bilney" by the other reformers.

John Foxe described this Fellow of Trinity College, who was in his early thirties. Foxe's portrait makes it clear that Bilney was known for reaching out to the most undesirable members of society:

> *This godly man, being a bachelor of law,*
> *was but of little stature and very slender of*

*body; and of a strait and temperate diet; and
given to good letters; and very fervent and stu-
dious in the Scriptures, as appeared by his sermons, his converting of sinners, his preaching at
the lazar cots [leper houses], wrapping them in
sheets, helping them of that they wanted, if
[hoping] they would convert to Christ; labori-
ous and painful to [going to great pains for] the
desperates; a preacher to the prisoners and
comfortless; a great doer in Cambridge, and a
great preacher in Suffolk and Norfolk."[1]*

While reading one of Erasmus's books in Latin, Bilney
discovered the doctrine of justification by faith. "Immediately, I seemed unto myself inwardly to feel a marvellous
comfort and quietness, insomuch as my bruised bones
leaped for joy," he later wrote.[2] His words and life had an
impact on two other leaders in Cambridge—Robert Barnes
and Hugh Latimer. Bilney shared Luther's distaste for a
religion based solely on external practices, but Bilney held
to the doctrines of papal supremacy and the authority of
the Roman Catholic Church.

In July 1525, Bilney was licensed to preach, but he
and the local friars sometimes disagreed. Twice he was
forcibly removed from the pulpit at Norwich while in
mid-sermon, creating quite a stir in the congregation. At
some point in 1526, he was questioned by Wolsey and
willingly swore not to hold or teach Luther's doctrines.

But in November 1527, Thomas Bilney was again
arrested and taken to London. This time, the situation
was more serious. He was charged with heresy and

brought before Bishop Tunstall and other bishops. Bilney did not understand why he was being questioned. He said that Luther was a detestable heretic and denied preaching Luther's doctrines. In spite of his protestations, Bilney was convicted of heresy in December 1527 and imprisoned in the Tower of London.

Bilney was not the only man brought in for questioning. In February 1528, Bishop Tunstall began a six-month campaign aimed at bringing in Lutheran sympathizers, Lollards, and anyone else who might present a threat to the church. By mid-March, the prisons were overflowing, a measure perhaps of how widely distributed Tyndale's Testament had become.

Tyndale's acquaintances in London drew attention as well. In May, Sir Thomas More sent for Humphrey Monmouth and interrogated him. He then sent him to the Tower of London. From his prison room, Monmouth appealed to King Henry, through Cardinal Wolsey, for clemency. He protested that although he had housed William Tyndale for six months about four and a half years earlier, Tyndale had always seemed to him to be a good priest, busily studying his books. It is not clear exactly when, but around the time that Monmouth was drawing unwelcome attention from the church authorities, he burned all the copies of Tyndale's sermons that had been left in his keeping so that they could not be used as evidence against him.

Word of the imprisonments reached Tyndale back in Germany. He had been working on the promised revision of his New Testament and was probably beginning his translation of the Old Testament. He was also toiling on the first work that would appear bearing his name as the author. Dated May 8, 1528, *The Parable of the Wicked Mammon* was Tyndale's response to what he hoped would be his last problem caused by William Roye, his former assistant.

The work Roye had been helping his friend Jerome Barlow create was a group of anti-Wolsey rhymes in English, entitled *Rede me and be not wroth.* The verse was satirical, recounting various events in England at the time, and pilloried Tunstall's attack on Tyndale's New Testament at St. Paul's Cross. It also compared Cardinal Wolsey to Pilate during the trial against Jesus and repeatedly attacked both Wolsey and Tunstall for "burning God's word, the holy testament."[3] Satires were popular at the time, but this work did not attack ideas or groups of people. It was very personal. The rhymes pointed specifically to both Cardinal Wolsey and Bishop Tunstall rather than aiming their barbs at the clergy in general. The first printing of the book opened with a drawing of Cardinal Wolsey with six axes. The cardinal's hat was colored red, and the axes had drops of red blood falling from them.

Because the printed book was unsigned, people in England and on the Continent tried to guess who was behind it. Not surprisingly, many pointed the finger at Tyndale and Roye, the two men well-known for having worked together on the English New Testament.

Tyndale was appalled. Such assumptions could do damage to God's Word and to the Protestant cause. They could diminish the credibility of both the English New Testament and the Old Testament translation on which he had begun work.

He felt it imperative to publicly disassociate himself from Roye and his writing. *The Parable of the Wicked Mammon* is based upon the parable of the unjust steward and borrows loosely from a sermon Martin Luther preached about the same parable. Drawing on several passages from the New Testament, it presents the reformers' teaching that faith is more important than works.

But in the prologue, entitled "William Tyndale otherwise called hychins to the reader," the English translator addressed the issue of William Roye. He briefly described his difficult experiences with his former assistant and how he warned Brother Jerome to avoid Roye. He also made a pointed argument against the approach used in *Rede me and be not wroth*: "Paul saith, the servant of the Lord must not strive, but be peaceable unto all men, and ready to teach, and one that can suffer the evil with meekness, and that can inform [instruct] them that resist, if God at any time will give them repentance for to know the truth. It becometh not then the Lord's servant to use railing rhymes, but God's word; which is the right weapon to slay sin, vice and all iniquity."[4]

Tyndale himself, however, was not beyond attacking the church establishment in general. In the closing paragraph of the prologue, he alluded to Christ charging the Pharisees with hypocrisy and then wrote, "There is no difference in the names between a pope, a cardinal, a bishop, and so forth, and to say a scribe, a Pharisee, a senior and so forth, but the thing is all one. . . . The old Antichrists brought Christ unto Pilate saying, by our law he ought to die. . . . They do all things of a good zeal, they say, they love you so well, that they had rather burn you than that you should have fellowship with Christ."[5]

Having settled matters to his satisfaction in the prologue, Tyndale proceeded to expound upon justification by faith. His imagery was dramatic as he warned that nothing but the shed blood of Jesus could save, "though thou hast a thousand holy candles about thee, a hundred ton of holy water, a ship-full of pardons, a cloth-sack full of friar's coats, and all the ceremonies in the world, and all the good works, deservings, and merits of all the men in the world, be they, or were they, never so holy."[6]

He went on to proclaim: "Christ is our Redeemer, Saviour, peace, atonement, and satisfaction to Godward for all the sin which they that repent (consenting to the law and believing the promises) do, have done, or shall do. So that if through fragility we fall a thousand times in a day, yet if we do repent again, we have alway mercy laid up for us in store in Jesus Christ our Lord."[7]

Once the work was completed, Tyndale found a printer—Johannes Hoochstraten of Antwerp. Printing was a huge industry in Antwerp, and Hoochstraten was quite skilled. Knowing that English and Low Country authorities were looking for those involved in producing Protestant materials in the English language, Hoochstraten quite willingly printed a false name and city for the printer of the book: Hans Luft of Marburg. Hans Luft was the name of a printer, but the real Hans Luft lived in Wittenburg. Tyndale would have had to leave Marburg by the spring of 1528 simply to find a printer. So identifying that city as the location of the printer would not lead officials to Tyndale's back door. Hoochstraten continued this deception in other books he printed for Tyndale.

Giving out such misinformation to mislead the authorities was a common practice. European printers were interested in making money, and nothing sold like Lutheran writings. Such books also attracted unwanted attention from agents of both church and state. Misdirecting these agents seemed the best way to keep both the money flowing in and one's business from being shut down. Many printers named Utopia as their place of business. Specifically Lutheran books sometimes claimed to be printed in Rome, at St. Peter's court.

Hoochstraten used one more technique to keep from being identified: He used a common typeface that most printers had access to, rather than using one of the more refined, and therefore identifiable, typefaces for which he was known.

Tyndale was right to be concerned about the consequences of Rowe and Barlow's *Rede me and be not wroth.* When it reached England, it provoked great anger among Wolsey, Tunstall, and their subordinates. Tyndale's own words against the church establishment in the prologue to *The Parable of the Wicked Mammon* did nothing to lessen tensions. That work reached England by June 1528, and when Wolsey and Tunstall managed to get a copy, they were livid. Archbishop Warham's council examined the book and proclaimed that it had more than two dozen heresies. Sir Thomas More called it "a book by which many have been beguiled and brought into many wicked heresies."[8]

On June 18, Cardinal Wolsey took direct action against the men he viewed as the ringleaders of the English

Lutherans living overseas. He ordered Sir John Hackett to demand that Princess Margaret, the regent of the Low Countries and aunt of the Holy Roman Emperor Charles V, arrest and deliver Tyndale, Roye, and an English merchant, Richard Herman.

Princess Margaret and her council replied that even Charles V could not extradite someone to England without a hearing. They promised to search for the three men, give them a hearing, and, if they were found guilty, to either punish them immediately or send them back to England. By July, Hackett was reporting that only Herman had been found, and that Hackett himself had seen the man thrown into prison. Herman was charged with supporting the English heretics in Antwerp, taking their books to England where he sold them, and thus encouraging rebellion against the king.

Cardinal Wolsey decided that more men should be assigned to the task of tracking down Tyndale and Roye. In August he sent John West, a friar from Greenwich who knew both Roye and Jerome Barlow. During the next month, another friar named Flegh joined West, and they set out for Cologne. Having no luck in that city, they made their way to the book fair at Frankfurt. Their letters back to England indicate that they thought Tyndale and Roye were still working together and that they did not know that the two men had parted company more than two and a half years earlier.

Meanwhile, the court in Antwerp was not pleased with the vagueness of the charges placed against Richard Herman. When the prisoner reasonably asked for the names of the Lutherans and rebels he was accused of helping and the dates on and methods with which he gave such assistance, Hackett wrote to Wolsey, begging for proof. No response came. Finally in January 1529, the prosecution produced two names. The court demanded more details, including dates, places, and methods, and because this information was not produced by February 5, the court ordered that Herman be released.

Wolsey may have failed to send the requested evidence against Herman because it didn't exist, or he may simply have been too absorbed by other events in England at the time. He continued actively seeking out people guilty of possessing "heretical" materials or beliefs. During the late summer of 1528, several young men from Cardinal College in Oxford, whom Wolsey had hand picked as students because of their intelligence, were arrested and imprisoned. Included in the group was John Frith, Tyndale's friend from his days in London. Frith was unexpectedly released later that year and in December escaped to the Continent. Three of the young men died from the filthy conditions in their prison.

That November, Thomas Bilney recanted the beliefs his accusers had settled against him, and after a year in the Tower of London, he was released by Wolsey to return to Cambridge. Apparently Bilney was quite depressed, possibly even suicidal, because he felt he had betrayed his principals. Concerned friends made sure that he was not left alone.

Wolsey was also in the midst of delicate negotiations over King Henry's request that the pope annul his marriage to Catherine of Aragon. His efforts had been ongoing for more than a year and were complicated by the fact that the queen was the aunt of Charles V who happened to be holding the pope captive. Queen Catherine did not want an annulment to her marriage, and Charles V sympathized with his aunt. Pope Clement VII, who had the power to grant Henry the desired annulment, did not want to antagonize his captor, which he certainly would do by proclaiming to the world that Catherine of Aragon was a common adulteress. Further, Henry was seeking the annulment by arguing that Scripture forbade marriage between a man and his brother's wife (Catherine was the widow of Henry's older brother Arthur), and the pope was reluctant to rule that an earlier pope had erred when he gave Henry special permission to marry Catherine.

On the other hand, both Francis I of France and King Henry had pledged to gain the pope's freedom, giving the pope incentive to be agreeable to Henry's request. So in the spring of 1528, he sent Cardinal Campeggio as his legate or representative to England. Campeggio's mission was to sit with Cardinal Wolsey and hear evidence about the validity of Henry's marriage. In a private message to Henry and Wolsey, Clement promised to abide by whatever conclusion Campeggio and Wolsey came to. This almost guaranteed Henry his long-desired annulment.

Concerned by Campeggio's mission, Charles V showed Pope Clement documents that he claimed proved Pope Leo had indeed validated through Scripture Henry's marriage to Queen Catherine. Pressured from both sides, Clement did what many leaders in similar situations have done throughout history. In October 1528, he sent a frantic message to Cardinal Campeggio, instructing him to find whatever means necessary to delay the proceedings.

The cardinal's first step was to try to convince Queen Catherine to retire to a nunnery. His thinking was that such a move would signal to Charles that his aunt was agreeable to her marriage ending, would remove the necessity of the hearing, and would extricate the pope from an impossible situation. It was a solution that had been used earlier when French King Louis XII had wanted to cast off his first wife. Queen Catherine agreed—on the condition that Henry likewise take monastic vows.

The last thing Henry was interested in was taking vows of poverty, obedience, and chastity. He was determined to rule England, marry Anne Boleyn, and produce a legitimate male heir. The queen's proposal would get nowhere, a fact which she likely knew quite well when she made it.

Working for a king who was growing increasingly impatient with the process of gaining an annulment and realizing that the king held him responsible for the success or failure of this process, Wolsey understandably may have had neither the time nor inclination to worry about Sir John Hackett's requests from the Continent.

While all this was happening, William Tyndale was keeping a low profile. Still, he was far from idle. By October 1528, he had completed what was probably his most influential book outside his Bible translations: *The Obedience of the Christian Man.* He obviously wrote it in response to charges that reformers were causing violence, such as the Peasants' War, in Europe. He wanted to make clear that subjects must obey their kings and that the reformers were not teaching people to revolt.

The Obedience of the Christian Man is divided into three sections. First comes a thirty-six page preface in which Tyndale encourages people who are being persecuted. Next an eight-page prologue explains what the book is meant to do. Finally, the body of the book explains various forms of obedience decreed by God, such as children to parents, servants to masters, wives to husbands, and citizens to their political rulers. It also explains the responsibilities of those who rule and are answerable to God for their decisions.

Tyndale included a special message to those reformers like Bilney who had recanted or denied their beliefs and felt such guilt about their decision: "If any man clean against his heart (but overcome with the weakness of the flesh), for fear of persecution, have denied, as Peter did, or have delivered his book, or put it away secretly; let him (if he repent), come again, and take better hold, and not despair, or take it for a sign that God hath forsaken him. For God ofttimes taketh His strength even from His very elect, when they either trust in their own strength, or are negligent to call to Him for His strength. And that doth He to teach them, and to make them feel, that in the fire of tribulation, for His word's sake, nothing can endure and abide save His work, and that strength only which He hath promised. For the which strength He will have us to pray unto Him night and day, with all instance."[9]

Once again, Tyndale made use of the printer Johannes Hoochstraten of Antwerp, who again misled authorities by identifying the printer as Hans Luft of Marburg. The book quickly made its way to England, and John Foxe recorded that Anne Boleyn received a copy. The story goes that she loaned it to one of the gentlewomen who attended her, Anne Gainsford. George Zouch, who was courting the gentlewoman, snatched it from her to gain her attention. But when he began reading the book, he was so impressed that he refused to return it. The dean of King Henry's chapel, noticing that Zouch was reading something during services and having been warned by Wolsey to be on the lookout for unsuitable books, seized the book from the young man and took it to Wolsey.

At this point, Anne Boleyn asked her maid to return the book, and the young woman fell on her knees and told the whole story of what had happened to it. Anne Boleyn, in turn, went to the king and asked his help in gaining the return of her book. He complied, she got her book back, and the king decided to read it for himself. He reportedly liked the book, probably because it asserted that God did not intend kings to be subservient to popes—an appealing idea when Henry's desire to provide a legitimate male heir for his nation was being thwarted by the church.

Whether the story is true or not (and it is impossible to corroborate it because there are no accounts from the time of Anne Boleyn that mention the event), Wolsey and other members of the church establishment were unanimous in their hatred of *The Obedience of the Christian Man*. Possession of the book became one of the primary "proofs" that a person was a heretic.

In January 1529, Tyndale's name was mentioned during open court in England in connection with heresy and rebellion. By February, a renewed search for him on the Continent had begun. Clearly the English translator needed to find a place to lie low. Antwerp would not work because Sir John Hackett was searching that city carefully. Marburg was now suspect because of its name being used on the published books. Rinck and West, two other English agents, were searching Antwerp, Cologne, and Frankfurt. Most experts agree that at this point Tyndale traveled to Hamburg. This position is based in part on John Foxe's account, but it is supported by other evidence as well.

Tyndale had been translating the Pentateuch, the first five books of the Old Testament, while he was working both on *The Parable of the Wicked Mammon* and on *The Obedience of the Christian Man.* He probably began learning Hebrew while at Wittenburg. (It is doubtful he began his Hebrew studies in England. Jews had been banished from England for more than two hundred years and the first professor of Hebrew joined the universities in 1524, the year Tyndale left England.) Not wanting to draw attention to himself in Antwerp, Tyndale took his completed Pentateuch, along with all his books, papers, and money, and caught a ship to Hamburg, the German port city at the mouth of the Elbe River.

Then tragedy struck. The ship wrecked along the coast of Holland, and Tyndale lost everything except his life. His translations were gone. Worse, all the reference books he used while wrestling with the Hebrew documents were lost. He had to begin all over again, starting with finding new copies of the books from which he worked. These would have included the Hebrew text, lexicons, and grammars, a copy of the Septuagint (a Greek translation of the

Hebrew Old Testament), and Latin and German translations of the Old Testament as well.

First, Tyndale caught another ship to Hamburg, where he stayed at the home of a respected widow and staunch Lutheran, Margaret van Emmerson. One of her sons had attended the University of Wittenberg back in 1524 when Tyndale had been there, and it is possible that the Englishman became acquainted with the family at that time. He also spent time with them in 1525 when he was completing his first translation of the English New Testament. Mrs. Van Emmerson was well known for her support of reformers, no matter what their nationality, and her home was often their base of operations.

Most scholars agree that Tyndale was met in Hamburg by Miles Coverdale, an Englishman who had been educated at Cambridge, where the two men may have first met. Coverdale was a few years older than Tyndale and a committed reformer. He quickly agreed to help Tyndale reconstruct his Pentateuch. While Coverdale couldn't help his friend much with the Hebrew and Greek, he was quite skilled in Latin, German, and French. Also, he would have provided Tyndale a much-needed partner with whom he could intelligently discuss some of the subtleties of translation.

From March through December of 1529, Tyndale redid his work on the Pentateuch in the relative safety of Hamburg. Because the city was a port, he also got frequent news of the political situation in England. As the year passed, it became clear that the attention of the English authorities was temporarily distracted from capturing Tyndale.

Chief among these distractions was the ongoing saga of King Henry and Anne Boleyn. Cardinal Campeggio, as instructed by Pope Clement, was doing a magnificent job of delaying the beginning of the hearings about the legitimacy of King Henry's marriage to Queen Catherine. On May 31, having run out of excuses, Campeggio and Wolsey opened the legatine court (so named because it was headed by the papal legate Campeggio). Catherine had appealed to Rome and refused to acknowledge the court's authority, but she did attend on the first day of the hearings. In dramatic fashion, she threw herself down on her knees in front of the king and pled for their marriage to continue.

King Henry raised Catherine to her feet and once again explained that he found no fault with her. He was taking this action because of dynastic and national concerns, and he rejected her appeal to Rome because the pope was still being held captive by Charles V. The queen left the room in tears and refused to participate in the hearings again.

Over the next several weeks, Cardinal Campeggio procrastinated skillfully. On July 23, he adjourned the court for the summer and "revoked" or referred the case to Rome. He quickly left England for that city. At about that same time, news would have reached England that Pope Clement had signed a treaty on June 29 that gained him his freedom on condition that he never agree to the annulment without Queen Catherine's willing consent.

Henry was enraged. Anne Boleyn complained that her youth was passing while cardinals took their time deciding the issue of annulment. She particularly blamed

Cardinal Wolsey for not doing more on the king's behalf, and King Henry began to share her resentment.

The cardinal was savvy enough a politician to realize that he was in a bad spot. Anne Boleyn did not like him, and if she became queen, she would make sure he lost his power. On the other hand, if he failed to gain the annulment, he would become the target of Henry's wrath. Besides, the man who had once been unassailable had now accrued too many enemies. The clergy hated Wolsey because of his tyrannical rule over them. The monks resented his seizure of some of their monasteries. Nobles blamed him for heavy taxes and were envious of his luxuriant lifestyle. Merchants hated Wolsey because he was behind the war with Charles that was cutting off important trade for them. Commoners saw the cardinal as the man who had sent too many of their sons to die in meaningless battles overseas. They all had dreams of a just end for the hated man. Clothiers from Kent suggested that he be put in a leaky boat and set adrift at sea.

In October 1529, King Henry had his lawyers charge Cardinal Wolsey with breaking an ancient British law by participating in the legatine court with Cardinal Campeggio. No one mentioned the fact that Wolsey had done this at the king's request. Wolsey threw himself on the king's mercy. The king stripped Wolsey of his chancellorship and laid claim to his palace in London, but he allowed Wolsey to leave London and remain archbishop of York.

Henry named Sir Thomas More the new lord chancellor. More was a vehement defender of the Roman Catholic Church, and in June of that year had published his *Dialogue Concerning Heresies,* a four-volume set that attacked Luther, Tyndale, and the English Bible in scathing terms. In November, the king and his new lord chancellor called Parliament into session. As news of these changes reached Tyndale in Hamburg, he realized it was probably safe enough to take his second translation of the Pentateuch to Antwerp for printing. The first book of the Bible, Genesis, came off the press on January 17, 1530, once again printed by Hoochstraten, alias Hans Luft of Marburg.

The Pentateuch made its way to England later that year and was often distributed as five individual books. It came to a nation where intolerance for Lutheran ideas was escalating. At the beginning of the year—at about the same time Genesis was coming off the press in Antwerp—a priest named Thomas Hitton was arrested in Kent, England, and charged with heresy. Hitton had spent time on the Continent, and English reformers there, including Tyndale, knew him.

During his hearing, he confessed that he had smuggled a New Testament into England. He was convicted by Archbishop Warham (the same man who had purchased the New Testaments in an effort to keep them out of circulation) and by Bishop Fisher of Rochester. On February 23, 1530, Thomas Hitton was burned alive at the stake, becoming the reformer's first English martyr.

When the Pentateuch arrived on England's shores, some of Tyndale's marginal notes gave his opponents more ammunition. At the end of Exodus eighteen, where Moses' father-in-law gives advice about the qualities to look for in leaders, Tyndale's translation reads, "Moreover seek out among all the people, men of activity which fear God, and men that are true and hate covetousness: and make them heads over the people" (v. 21). In the margin, Tyndale noted, "Our prelates neither fear God, for they preach not his word truly: nor are less covetous than Judas: for they have received of the devil the kingdoms of the earth and the glory thereof which Christ refused. Mat. 4."[10]

Numbers twenty-three continues the story of Balaam confronting the rulers of Moab. In Tyndale's translation, Balaam asks, "How shall I curse whom God curseth not and how shall I defy whom the Lord defieth not?" (v. 8). Tyndale's marginal note is short and to the point: "The pope can tell how."[11]

Both in England and on the Continent, attitudes toward reformers were hardening. On May 25, King Henry personally denounced both *The Parable of the Wicked Mammon* and *The Obedience of the Christian Man*. He demanded that all such books be turned in within fifteen days. Bishop Tunstall oversaw another bonfire of books at St. Paul's Cross, shortly before he was transferred to another bishopric and replaced with the more brutal Bishop John Stokesley. Holy Roman Emperor Charles V ordered all copies of the New Testament in any language to be surrendered and the printing of them to be stopped. Convicted heretics were regularly condemned to death either by sword, fire, or live burial.

Little hard evidence was needed for a person to be investigated. John and Cecily Eaton were persecuted for being noticed by unnamed persons of their parish holding down their heads in church and not looking at the sacrament during mass. In August 1530, a man was arrested for believing that the church service in England should be spoken in English rather than Latin. His wife, sisters, and father testified against him.

In such an environment, no place was entirely safe for William Tyndale. Except for occasional trips to other cities in northern Europe, he probably stayed in Antwerp for the next four years. Although Antwerp had a large English community and many printers, it was no haven to reformers. On December 7, 1529, an edict was issued, stating in part: "That nobody should presume from that time forwards to write, print, or cause to be written or printed any new book upon what subject soever, without having first obtained letters of licence for the said purpose; on pain of being piloried, and marked besides with a red-hot iron, or an eye put out, or a hand cut off according to the discretion of the judge, who is to see the sentence executed without delay or mercy."[12]

But the problems Tyndale saw in the church combined with the increased persecution of reformers during 1530 led him to write *The Practice of Prelates. Whether the King's grace may be separated from his queen because she was his brother's wife*. While the small book did address the controversial issue of Henry VIII's quest for an annulment—Tyndale concluded that the marriage between the king and Queen Catherine was binding and could not be dissolved in the eyes of God—it went much further.

Using the specific example of Wolsey's and other church leader's efforts to facilitate the divorce and use the action to their advantage, Tyndale launched into an attack on how the clergy and the papal establishment had become corrupted, thoroughly entangled in the world's political situation rather than in the things of God.

Even the title communicated more in 1530 than it does today. The word *practice* in Tyndale's time carried with it the idea of scheming through trickery. Tyndale biographer David Daniell compares the translator's use of the word to Shakespeare's:

> "*The poisoned and dying Laertes says 'The foul practice hath turned itself on me' (Hamlet V.ii.309); and 'This is practice, Gloucester,' says Goneril to the fallen and dying Edmund (King Lear V.iii.151). 'By the law of war thou wast not bound to answer/An unknown opposite . . .' Shakespeare clearly associated the word with trickery that is lethal.*"[13]

Tyndale's readers would have glanced at the title and immediately understood that *The Practice of Prelates* was an indictment of the underhanded scheming of church leaders.

Satire was one of Tyndale's favorite tools in this book. After spending pages describing the sins and excesses of Charlemagne, who began the Holy Roman Empire seven hundred years before Tyndale's time, the Englishman wrote, "And there he lieth and is a saint as right is."[14]

The Practice of Prelates, once again claiming to be printed by Hans Luft of Marburg, came off the presses belonging to Johannes Hoochstraten during the fall of 1530. It was not designed to appease the enemies of reform, and as could be expected, when the little book began arriving in England later that year, it added fuel to an already raging fire.

eight

The Practice of Prelates had such impact on life in London that both the ambassador from Milan and the ambassador from the Holy Roman Empire reported back to their countries about it in December 1530. They undoubtedly would have mentioned the book anyway because it dealt with the highly controversial issue of King Henry's marriage to Catherine of Aragon and supported the position held by Charles V. But the ambassadors felt the reaction of English authorities to Tyndale's work was worth mentioning as well.

The ambassador from Milan reported that three thousand copies of the book were circulating in England and that it was written by an Englishman of great learning named Tindaro or Tyndal. Both ambassadors reported that large signs were put up throughout the city, both denouncing *The Practice of Prelates* and announcing that the English universities were in favor of the divorce. The rule that "any publicity is good publicity" was in force even five hundred years ago, and these signs simply increased interest in the book. Chapuys, the ambassador from the Holy Roman Empire, noted that a few days after the signs went up they came back down. He concluded that this was either because the king was afraid Tyndale would respond to the signs or because someone figured out that free publicity for the books would only increase public interest in them.

Chapuys also described merchants being charged with possession of the books with the intent to sell them. These men, including Tyndale's brother John, were arrested in mid-November and then marched through London's streets on market day. They were forced to wear mitered caps of pasteboard that announced their crime: "I have sinned against the commandments of the king." Tied around their necks were copies of *The Practice of Prelates*, and after the march was completed, the merchants threw these books into a prepared fire in the Cheap, London's huge marketplace. The ambassador thought this punishment would only draw more attention to the reviled writings.

He then reported that he had it on the best authority that the king, "afraid lest the priest Tyndale shall write more boldly against him, and hoping to persuade him to retract what he has already written, has invited him back to England, and offered him several good appointments and a seat in his council."[1]

Where did such an idea come from? Quite possibly from Thomas Cromwell. The son of a brewer, fuller, and blacksmith, Cromwell had risen to the position of Thomas Wolsey's right-hand man. He escaped the king's disfavor when charges were brought against Wolsey in 1529 and had gained a seat on the royal council. Henry continued to trust the man, even after Wolsey was charged with treason during the fall of 1530. (Wolsey died from dysentery on his way back to London for the trial.)

Cromwell was both efficient and effective. He was able to take Henry's visions for the country and make them reality. He had a gift both for getting things done in the present and being able to see future implications of those actions. Cromwell was also flexible, and already Lord Chancellor Thomas More was showing signs of being more loyal to the church than to Henry's wishes in the issue of divorce. Henry appreciated having an advisor who wasn't as tightly married to principle as Sir Thomas More.

Whether King Henry or Thomas Cromwell thought of it first, they agreed on the idea that it would be better to have Tyndale writing from within England where they would have tighter control over his words than to live with a situation in which he continued to send inflammatory books to England from across the North Sea. Near the end of November 1530, Cromwell sent Stephen Vaughan to the Continent on a delicate mission. He was to find William Tyndale and offer him safe conduct back to England.

Cromwell had known Vaughan for a while. The king's factor, or trade representative, in the Low Countries, Vaughan had run unusual errands for Cromwell in the past. Faced with this new mission, he sent letters to Tyndale in Frankfurt, Hamburg, and Marburg, the three cities most often rumored to contain the elusive English translator. In them he presented the king's offer of a safe conduct to England. On January 26, 1531, Vaughan wrote to the king that he had failed to locate Tyndale but had received a reply to his letters. Tyndale had refused the offer both because he felt England was not a safe place for him and because he suspected that the offer was a trap. (And not without cause—during the previous hundred years, men had died in "accidents" while traveling under guarantees of safe conduct.)

On April 18, 1531, Vaughan again wrote to King Henry. He had an incredible story to relay. A messenger had come to him saying a friend of Vaughan's desired to speak with him. The messenger said he did not know the name of the friend but that he would take Vaughan to him. Dubious, the Englishman followed the messenger to a field outside the gates of Antwerp. He understood that if a king's agent did not take such risks, he might miss out on important information.

Arriving at the field, a man came up to him and said, "Do you not know me?" Vaughan replied that he couldn't place him. Then the man said, "My name is Tyndale."

Vaughan was stunned. "But Tyndale!" he exclaimed, "fortunate be our meeting." The two men proceeded to talk about many issues, including Tyndale's distress that the king disliked *The Practice of Prelates,* "considering that in it I did but warn his grace of the subtle demeanour of the clergy of his realm towards his person, and of the shameful abusions by them practised, not a little threatening the displeasure of his grace and weal of his realm: in which doing I showed and declared the heart of a true

144

subject, which sought the safeguard of his royal person and weal of his commons, to the intent that his grace, thereof warned, might in due time prepare his remedies against their subtle dreams."

Vaughan further reported that he tried to convince Tyndale to travel to England. "But to this he answered, that he neither would nor durst come into England, albeit your grace would promise him never so much the surety: fearing lest, as he hath before written, your promise made should surely be broken, by the persuasion of the clergy, which would affirm that promises made with heretics ought not to be kept."[2]

The men also discussed Tyndale's response to Sir Thomas More's *Dialogue Concerning Heresies*, a four-volume work which had attacked both Luther and Tyndale. In 1531, two years after More's work first appeared, Tyndale had completed his *Answer unto Sir T. Mores Dialogue*. The heart of the issue from Tyndale's perspective was that Scripture should be used to judge the church's doctrine and practice. In the prologue, he wrote:

> *Judge therefore reader whether the pope with his be the church, whether their authority be above the scripture, whether all they teach without scripture be equal with the scripture, whether they have erred and not only whether they can. . . . Judge whether it be possible that any good should come out of their dumb [silent] ceremonies and sacraments into thy soul. Judge their penance, pilgrimages, pardons, purgatory, praying to posts, dumb blessings, dumb absolutions,*

> *their dumb pattering, and howling, their*
> *dumb strange holy gestures, with all their*
> *dumb disguisings, their satisfactions and*
> *justifyings.[3]*

As the discussion between Tyndale and Vaughan continued, Vaughan reported that Tyndale began to seem nervous about being in such an isolated location with a representative from the king. Evening was coming, and Tyndale took his leave, heading down the road away from Antwerp. Vaughan himself returned to the city, trusting Tyndale's promise that they would meet again. He assumed that Tyndale circled around and returned to the city another way. With his report, he sent to the king a copy of Tyndale's response to More.

In fact, Tyndale and Vaughan met two more times. On May 20, Vaughan reported in a letter to Cromwell that he had met with Tyndale and again asked him to return to England. This time Tyndale proposed a deal: "If it would stand with the king's most gracious pleasure to grant only a bare text of the scripture to be out forth among his people, like as is put forth among the subjects of the emperor in these parts, and of other Christian princes, be it of the translation of what person soever shall please his majesty, I shall immediately make faithful promise never to write more, not abide two days in these parts after the same: but immediately to repair unto his realm, and there most humbly submit myself at the feet of his royal majesty, offering my body to suffer what pain or torture, yea, what death his grace will, so this be obtained. And till that time, I will abide the asperity of

146

all chances, whatsoever shall come, and endure my life in as many pains as it is able to bear and suffer."[4]

Tyndale was offering to return to England, stop writing books, and submit to any kind of punishment including a painful death if only Henry would release an English Bible to his people. So committed was Tyndale to the idea of his English ploughman being able to hear the Bible in his own language that he did not care who the king chose to do the translation, nor did he object to it being released in "bare text"—that is without notes. He pointed out that this was no less than what Charles V had allowed throughout the Holy Roman Empire.

Vaughan's third meeting with Tyndale took place sometime in June. In a letter to Cromwell written on June 19, Vaughan reported that he had repeated "what the king's royal pleasure was, but I find him always singing one note." Simply put, Tyndale refused either to return to England or to stop writing books until King Henry authorized an English Bible. Shortly after this letter was written, Vaughan returned to England.

Tyndale was wise not to jump at King Henry's offer. The escalating persecution of English reformers in 1530 continued throughout 1531, and news of these actions no doubt reached Tyndale in Europe. Some of the news came from John Frith, the young mathematician whom Tyndale had spent time with during his London days. Frith traveled to England during Lent 1531 and returned to Antwerp with news for Tyndale.

The new bishop of London, John Stokesley, sought out reformers more aggressively than had Bishop Tunstall before him. Skinners, glaziers, servants, tailors, harpers, bookbinders, weavers, priests, and people from many other professions and trades were being arrested simply for possessing the New Testament in English or any number of other books printed in Antwerp. During the spring of 1531, Stokesley had Thomas Bilney, Hugh Latimer, and Richard Bayfield arrested again, and he reintroduced the burning alive of men and women convicted of heresy. Latimer was released, but Bilney and Bayfield remained in the Tower, awaiting trial.

Ever since his earlier release from prison in December 1529, Bilney had been tormented by feelings that he had betrayed his principles. In 1530, he began preaching in Norfolk and gave the anchoress (or woman hermit) of Norwich a copy of the English New Testament. The Bishop of Norwich (presumably working under orders from Stokesley) sent officers to arrest Bilney. He was charged, condemned, removed from the priesthood, and then handed over to secular authorities.

When John Frith reached the Continent, Bilney was in prison awaiting his execution. Frith himself returned to England for unknown reasons that July. He was jailed, released, and then spent weeks wearing various disguises and trying to find a way out of the country. He didn't succeed. Agents of both the crown and Bishop Stokesley arrested Frith and put him in the Tower of London where he was given the consideration of not having to wear shackles. This stood in contrast to Richard Bayfield's more typical treatment in the Tower at the same time. He was held to the wall of his cell by his neck, waist, and legs and often left in total darkness for days at a time. Frith stayed in the Tower for five months.

Meanwhile, others were being executed for their beliefs. In August 1531 Thomas Bilney was burned at the stake in Norwich. The site of his execution had been a common place for earlier burnings of Lollards, and the case became quite well known throughout England.

Richard Bayfield, who also had attended Cambridge, was burned alive that December. He had been arrested before and recanted his beliefs. Thomas More wrote of him, "After that like a dog returning to his vomit, and being fled over the sea, and sending from thence Tyndale's heresies thither with many mischievous sorts of books." More concluded his comments by adding, "Of Bayfield's burning hath Tyndale no great cause to glory."[5]

Tyndale was grieved, although not surprised, by the increasing hostility of the English church toward reformers, and he did what he could to encourage his friends who were suffering. He wrote two letters to John Frith while the brilliant mathematician continued waiting in the Tower to learn his fate. In the first letter, Tyndale gave advice about how Frith should answer his critics:

> *Finally, if there were in me any gift that could help at hand, and aid you if need required, I promise you I would not be far off, and commit the end to God. My soul is not faint, though my body be weary. But God hath made me evil-favoured in this world, and without grace in the sight of men, speechless and rude, dull and slow-witted: your part shall be to supply what lacketh in me; remembering that as lowliness of heart shall make you high with*

God, even so meekness of words shall make you
sink into the hearts of men. Nature giveth age
authority, but meekness is the glory of youth,
and giveth them honour. Abundance of love
maketh me exceed in babbling.[6]

In his second letter, Tyndale encouraged his good friend to be faithful to God and know that he was not alone in his sufferings. He also mentioned Frith's wife, with whom he had been in contact. "Sir, your wife is well content with the will of God, and would not, for her sake, have the glory of God hindered."[7]

While in the Tower, Frith was able to write, and he completed a work that argued against some of Thomas More's positions. In it, he included these words about William Tyndale:

And Tyndale, I trust, liveth, well content with
such a poor apostle's life, as God gave his son
Christ and his faithful ministers in this world,
which is not sure of so many mites as ye [More]
be yearly of pounds, although I am sure that for
his learning and judgment in scripture he were
more worthy to be promoted than all the bishops
in England. I received a letter from him, which
was written since Christmas, wherein among
other matters he writeth thus: —I call God to
record, against the day we shall appear before
our Lord Jesus to give a reckoning of our
doings, that I never altered one syllable of
God's word against my conscience, nor would

*do this day, if all that is in the earth, whether it
be honour, pleasure, or riches, might be given
me. Moreover I take God to record to my conscience, that I desire of God to myself in this
world no more than that, without which I cannot
keep his laws etc. Judge, Christian reader,
whether these words be not spoken of a faithful,
clear, innocent heart. And as for his behaviour,
[it] is such that I am sure no man can reprove
him of any sin; howbeit no man is innocent
before God, which beholdeth the heart.*[8]

Frith's writings were done carefully, however. Apparently he was allowed to visit with friends, and in this
way Frith both received writing supplies and smuggled
his manuscripts out of the Tower. But Frith had to watch
out for those in authority. In one of his books he wrote,
"I may not have such books as are necessary for me, neither yet pen, ink, nor paper, but only secretly, so that I
am in continual fear both of the lieutenant and of my
keeper, lest they should espy any such thing by me; and
therefore it is little marvel that the work be imperfect, for
whensoever I hear the keys ring at the door, straight all
must be conveyed out of the way; and then if any notable
thing had been in my mind, it was clean lost."[9]

Frith could not remain in the Tower indefinitely. During Lent 1532, a royal chaplain brought the situation to
King Henry's attention, who in turn ordered that Frith be
tried. His trial was held over several days at Archbishop
Thomas Cranmer's home at Croyden. Frith turned back all
attempts to get him to change his positions, so on June 20,

1532, he was brought before Bishop Stokesley at St. Paul's Cathedral. The bishop found him guilty and turned him over to secular authorities for punishment. On July 4, John Frith was burned alive at the stake in Smithfield, England.

As the months passed and Tyndale learned of the deaths of these friends, he must have been relieved that he'd refused the king's guarantee of safe conduct to return to England. That offer was now withdrawn. If Tyndale would not return willingly, the king was determined to have him arrested and extradited. He ordered his ambassador to the Holy Roman Empire to ask Charles V to find Tyndale and hand him over. Charles was well aware that his aunt, Queen Catherine, had been removed from the London court and forced to return her royal jewels so that Henry could give them to Anne Boleyn. He was not inclined to do the English king any favors. Besides, in *The Practice of Prelates,* Tyndale had defended Queen Catherine's position on the legitimacy of her marriage to Henry. Then again, it would be as difficult for Charles to track down Tyndale as it had been for Henry. So the emperor sent a polite note to Henry, explaining that he had no proof that Tyndale had broken any laws in England or in the empire.

Not to be put off, Henry next ordered Sir Thomas Elyot to find Tyndale, kidnap him (thereby avoiding the necessity of having him tried under Charles's authority), and return him to England. Elyot understood how difficult this task was. Many skilled men had tried to accomplish the same thing before him and had failed. In a letter written to the duke of Norfolk on March 14, 1532, Elyot stated of Tyndale, "His person [is] uncertain to come by."[10]

In spite of the acknowledged difficulties of his task, Thomas Elyot made a concerted effort. He spent the king's money lavishly in efforts to bribe people. He loitered around print shops and gossiped with the workers. He followed every lead he received. By June, however, Elyot had given up. He resigned his post and returned to England without Tyndale.

Tyndale was aware of these attempts to bring him into custody. When he was not carefully avoiding the king's agents, he was busy with the continued revision of his translation of the New Testament, as well as the translation of more books of the Old Testament such as Jonah, Joshua, Judges, Ruth, 1 and 2 Samuel, 1 and 2 Kings, and 1 and 2 Chronicles. Perhaps he sensed time was running out. Tyndale chose not to respond to Sir Thomas More's six-volume *Confutation,* published in 1532 and 1533, which again attacked Tyndale's writings. Instead he focused his energies on completing his task for the English ploughman, translating the entire Bible into English.

As he worked, word drifted across from England that King Henry was using Parliament to weaken the power of the pope over the English church. In 1532, what became known as the "Reformation Parliament" passed laws that made clergy under the rank of subdeacon subject to civil rather than religious courts when charged with a felony. The new laws also reduced fees and fines the religious courts could charge, as well as the fees the church charged for services it provided. They stopped the flow of English money to Rome in payment for dispensations, indulgences, and other services the pope administered. The laws also ended the practice of sending annates (the first year's revenues of a new bishop or other high-ranking church official) to the pope.

In March of that year, the Convocation (a meeting of English bishops and other high-ranking officials) determined that it was ready to break with the Roman Catholic Church: "May it please your Grace to cause the said unjust exactions to cease. . . . And in case the Pope will make process against this realm for the attaining these annates . . . may it please your Highness to ordain in the present Parliament that the obedience of your Highness and of the people be withdrawn from the See of Rome," they proclaimed.[11]

The Convocation went even further when, on May 15, 1532, it pledged to submit all its future laws to a committee, half of which would be made up of laypeople. This committee would have the power to veto any church law it judged to be harmful to the realm. In effect, the Reformation Parliament and the 1532 Convocation created the Church of England as an arm of the English government and subject to the state rather than to Rome. Thomas More, always loyal to the Roman Catholic Church, resigned as lord chancellor the next day and retired to his home.

Henry soon had reason to want to force the annulment issue. Unknown to the general public, Anne Boleyn became pregnant. Henry married her secretly on January 15, 1533, and asked Pope Clement one last time for an annulment. The pope refused. Things began to move quickly. Henry next turned to the Convocation, which in April approved his divorce. Thomas Cranmer, now Archbishop of Canterbury, declared Henry's marriage with Catherine null and void on May 23. Five days later, Cranmer proclaimed Anne to be Henry's lawful wife. On May 31, Anne, dressed in brocade and jewels, was crowned Queen of England. The crowds lining the streets, watching the stately pageant, were noticeably silent. Queen Catherine still owned the hearts of the English people.

Pope Clement, as expected, pronounced the new marriage null and void, said that its future offspring would be illegitimate, and excommunicated Henry. On September 7, 1533, the only child born to Henry and Anne arrived. They named the red-headed princess Elizabeth.

The change in England's relationship to Rome did not significantly affect what was being taught in the churches. Theologically, Henry was a Roman Catholic, so he set out both to punish Protestant critics of Catholic teachings and Catholic critics of his role as head of the English church. Nothing he said or did raised hopes that England might soon have an authorized English translation of the Bible.

As 1533 drew to a close, Tyndale was nearing completion of the revisions to the New Testament that he had promised his readers seven years before. The new edition was published by Martin de Keyser in Antwerp the next year as a six-inch tall, four-inch wide, one-and-a-half-inch thick, four hundred page book. But before the New Testament could be finished, Tyndale faced an unexpected problem.

The Antwerp printer Christopher von Endhoven had been publishing pirated copies of Tyndale's New Testament since the end of 1526. He was imprisoned in

England in 1531 on charges of selling the New Testament and died there. Meanwhile, his widow had continued his printing business in Antwerp, and one of her customers was a graduate of Cambridge named George Joye. At the end of 1533 or the beginning of 1534, Mrs. von Endhoven asked Joye to oversee the fourth edition of their pirated English New Testament.

No one knows exactly how much work Joye did on this edition. Given that he was working with non-English-reading printers and that English spelling itself was not yet standardized, there could have been a huge number of spelling or punctuation errors that had to be corrected. This in itself would not have bothered Tyndale. His feelings about the previous pirated editions of the New Testament are not known. Even if he had opposed such efforts (and an argument can be made that he would have been glad to get any English-language Testaments into England, no matter what the source), he never wrote about them one way or another. Besides, no copyright laws existed to protect his work.

Unfortunately, however, Joye did not understand his own limitations. He had a good command of Latin, but his knowledge of Greek was poor, and nothing indicates that he had training in Hebrew. In his biography of Tyndale, David Daniell describes four serious blunders Joye made in the process of overseeing the von Endhoven printing:

> *First, he had beside him a Vulgate, in order*
> *to check Tyndale's accuracy; precisely as if*
> *Jerome were after all the true text and*

*Erasmus's Greek text (from which Tyndale
worked) a sport. Joye did not have much Greek,
and he was, if you please, "correcting" the
work of one of the most formidable Greek scholars of the time. Second, he took it upon himself
to make silent substantive changes, like making
Jesus say to Peter in Matthew 16, "Thou art
Stone. And upon this same stone . . ." Third, and
with breathtaking folly, he "corrected"
Tyndale's theology at that point of importance,
the word "resurrection," changing it in twenty
places to "the life after this life" or whatever. . . .
Finally, all this was done silently, appearing
under Tyndale's name on the title-page, without
bothering to inform Tyndale, his neighbour, col-
league, fellow-exile and Christian brother, that
he was doing it.[12]*

Tyndale was horrified. Just as his own revised version of the New Testament was set to be printed, an
edition was entering circulation with his name on it but
presenting views that were not his at all. He hurriedly
wrote more than eight pages that formed a second prologue to his 1534 New Testament. In it he explained
what George Joye had done and outlined his objections
to the edition:

*But when the printing of mine was almost
finished, one brought me a copy and shewed me
so many places, in such wise altered that I was
astonied and wondered not a little what fury*

had driven him to make such change and to call it a diligent correction. For throughout Matthew, Mark and Luke perpetually: and oft in the Acts, and sometime in John and also in the Hebrews, where he findeth this word resurrection, he changeth it into the life after this life, or very life, and such like, as one that abhorred the name of the resurrection.

If that change, to turn resurrection into life after this life, be a diligent correction, then must my translation be faulty in those places, and saint Jerome's, and all the translators that ever I heard of in what tongue soever it be, from the apostles unto this his diligent correction (as he calleth it) which whether it be so or no, I permit it to other men's judgements.

But of this I challenge George Joye, that he did not put his own name thereto and call it rather his own translation: and that he playeth boo peep, and in some of his books putteth in his name and title, and in some keepeth it out. It is lawful for who will to translate and show his mind, though a thousand had translated before him. But it is not lawful (thinketh me) nor yet expedient for the edifying of the unity of the faith of Christ, that whosoever will, shall by his own authority, take another man's translation and put out and in and change at pleaseure, and call it a correction.

Moreover, ye shall understand the George Joye hath had of a long time marvellous imaginations

about this word resurrection, that it should be
taken for the state of souls after their departing
from their bodies, and hath also (though he hath
been reasoned with thereof and desired to cease)
yet sown his doctrine by secret letters on that side
the sea, and caused great division among the
brethren.[13]

Tyndale then went into a lengthy discussion of the resurrection, quoting from numerous passages in the New Testament. He concluded his second prologue by including the printer's identifying material that appeared in the pirated copy so that readers could distinguish Tyndale's work from Joye's.

Tyndale's revised New Testament did much more than correct typographical errors from the 1526 Worms edition. In the eight years between editions, he had become even better versed in Greek and Hebrew. His work on the Pentateuch and other parts of the Old Testament influenced his revisions of the New Testament. Many places in the Gospels include a Greek translation of passages from the Hebrew Old Testament, such as when Old Testament prophecies are being quoted. This is true also of some of the epistles, especially Hebrews. In such cases, Tyndale referred back to the original Hebrew and used his understanding of that language to help him better represent what was being said.

Committed as he was both to finding the perfect English word to convey the original Greek meaning and to placing his words in an order that would create the strongest effect, Tyndale made seemingly minor changes that added significantly to the overall quality of the translation. David Daniell cites several examples, including these:

> *"Blessed are the maintainers of peace"*
> *in Matthew five becomes "Blessed are the*
> *peacemakers."*

> *"Each day's trouble is sufficient for the self*
> *same day" at the end of Matthew six becomes*
> *"For the day present hath ever enough of his*
> *own trouble."*

> *"Which would proffer his son a stone if he*
> *asked him bread" in Matthew seven becomes*
> *"If his son asked him bread, would he offer*
> *him a stone?"[14]*

Tyndale also included short introductions to each book except Acts and Revelation. Being able to insert cross-references and marginal notes must have been a special joy to the translator who had been forced to remove all such helps from his Worms edition. The tone of the notes is much more moderate than those used in the Pentateuch, and pointed comments directed at the clergy have all but disappeared.

Tyndale made more than five thousand changes in his 1534 New Testament. A deluxe special edition, featuring vellum pages, gilt edges, and colored illustrations was presented to Queen Anne, who was known to be sympathetic to the reformers.

As the 1534 New Testament made its way to England, it was landing on the shores of a nation quite changed during the eight years since the 1526 edition had appeared. Cardinal Wolsey was dead, and his replacement, Thomas More, had retired and was in danger of arrest because of his views on the King's marriage. Queen Catherine had been banished from London, and a new queen reigned in her place. Princess Mary had been declared illegitimate and was kept in a castle away from either of her parents. The infant Princess Elizabeth was blissfully unaware of the political turmoil surrounding her that would ultimately lead her both to the Tower of London and the British throne. And clergy throughout the land were becoming accustomed to looking to their king rather than to the pope for spiritual leadership.

With all these changes, some wondered how long opposition to an English Bible would last. William Tyndale only understood that his work was half done. Much of the Old Testament remained to be translated, and as God gave him breath, he would work to complete the task.

nine

I n the spring of 1535, William Tyndale was living in relative safety and comfort in Antwerp. For about a year, he had been the guest of Thomas Poyntz, a successful English businessman and a relative of Lady Walsh, at whose home in Little Sodbury Manor Tyndale had worked. Poyntz lived in Antwerp, along with his wife and family, in what was known as the English House. They shared these accommodations with a number of other English merchants who had business contacts throughout Europe.

Since trade with England generated a considerable amount of money for Antwerp, the city's political leaders protected the residents of the English House against the growing anti-English and anti-Reformation hostility of Roman Catholic leaders in nearby Brussels and Louvain.

His merchant friends in the English House provided

Tyndale with a regular and substantial income. For probably the first time in his adult life, William Tyndale had as much money as he needed for books, paper, quill pens, ink, and, most importantly, an unlimited supply of candles. He could afford to pay others to help him with the work of translation. When his finished work was submitted to a printer, Tyndale could share in the printing costs. This meant that more copies of a book or pamphlet could be printed and distributed than if the printer were bearing all the costs alone.

His new financial situation also allowed him to give away substantial sums of money to the poor. He regularly spent two days a week in this work. Mondays were particularly important to Tyndale because that was the day he visited poor English refugees, who, like himself, had come to Antwerp to escape religious persecution.

To the English community in Antwerp and to others who supported the principles of the Reformation, Tyndale was something of a celebrity. He was often invited to dinner by friends in the English House, reformers in Antwerp, or curious English visitors who wished to meet the man who had translated the New Testament into their native language. On Sundays, Tyndale would join his friends for informal worship services, where he would read short passages of Scripture and comment on them.

Even with his other commitments, the work of translation was still the center of his life. Tyndale's 1534 New Testament had demonstrated a mature scholarship in Greek, and he was continuing to make improvements to it.

In the process of translating the Pentateuch into clear and direct English, Tyndale had become one of the most important Hebrew scholars in Europe. During his time with the Poyntz family, he probably finished his work on the historical books of Joshua through 2 Chronicles and was beginning work on Ezra, Nehemiah, and Esther. It is likely that he was also looking forward to the immense challenges and opportunities offered by Job and the Psalms, as well as the complex issues dealt with in the longest prophetic books of the Old Testament—Isaiah, Jeremiah, Ezekiel, and Daniel. Many passages from the Psalms and the Prophets had already been examined by him in the process of translating the New Testament.

Even with so much going well, no one in the English House felt entirely safe.

Thomas Poyntz and the other merchants were international businessmen. Their economic survival depended on understanding the currents of change reshaping the map of Europe. They were well aware of how rapidly the beliefs of the Protestant Reformation were spreading across Europe. In many cases they had witnessed firsthand the violence generated by the conflict.

Even William Tyndale, who is sometimes portrayed as a naive scholar with little practical knowledge of the world around him, understood the political and personal implications of religious conflicts. He had, after all, spent most of his life studying the Bible. Both the tortured history of Israel in the Old Testament and the deadly religious opposition faced by Jesus and His disciples in the New Testament taught the same lesson. Established religious authorities do not quietly accept challenges to their power, even in the name of faithfulness to God.

Tyndale's experiences at Oxford and Cambridge, as well as the controversy he had stirred up at Little Sodbury Manor and his inability to get official support for his work of translation in London had all reinforced this lesson. In the end, the religious conflicts in England made him a political exile.

After leaving England, he could have retreated to a quiet life of scholarly studies, perhaps in Wittenberg or some other Lutheran stronghold, and waited for the religious climate to change. Instead, he became an activist who was determined to make the Bible widely available in English. At the same time, he became an advocate for reforming a self-serving religious system that cared more about its own power and wealth than about the spiritual lives of people for whom Christ died.

Rejecting a life of scholarly isolation, Tyndale embraced conflict and personal danger. He was forced to flee from Cologne while printing his first edition of the New Testament in 1525. After his translation appeared in 1526, he was a marked man, and the dangers he faced only increased as his opposition to the religious status quo became better known.

In *The Obedience of Christian Man* (1528), Tyndale encouraged individual Christians to make the Bible itself their guide for moral living and social order. In *The Practice of Prelates* (1530), he confronted the theological and moral corruption of the Roman Catholic Church, particularly as it was exemplified in the power-hungry scheming of Wolsey. When viciously attacked by Thomas More in 1531, Tyndale vigorously defended both himself and the principles of the reformers.

He was also an active distributor of his own writings. Here, Tyndale drew upon his practical knowledge of trade that he had gained growing up in the Severn River Valley, one of the most active markets in Western Europe. It was no accident that his patrons in Antwerp were merchants. For years, Tyndale had used his contacts with various businessmen to smuggle his writing into England.

Tyndale stayed in contact with fellow reformers in England and on the Continent by letter and through mutual friends. He had already seen many of them die for their convictions.

Everyone in the English House understood the risks they were running, even in Antwerp, by actively supporting the reformers. But they were watching for a direct attack from the authorities in Brussels or Louvain, one their friends in the city government would quickly warn them against.

No one understood that while their attention was focused on the Roman Catholic Church and the Holy Roman Empire, another threat was approaching unseen. It was financed and organized by English religious leaders opposed to the principles of the Reformation, and its targets were the most important reformers among the English community in Antwerp.

The primary agent of this plot was a young Englishman from a wealthy and respected family, the Oxford-educated Henry Phillips. He was the third son born into his family at a time when elder brothers usually inherited most of a family's wealth and political power. Both his position as a younger son and the Oxford education he received strongly suggest that his parents were preparing him for an influential career in the church. The fact that senior church officials had consented to be his patrons also reinforces this idea. They would guide him through the ordination process, arrange for his first assignments in the church, and provide direct financial support.

But sometime between his graduation in February 1533 and the spring of 1535, he became an outcast from his own family. Henry Phillips was given money by his father to deliver to someone in London, but the money never arrived. Instead, the young Oxford graduate gambled with it and lost everything. Phillips tried to find a way out of his situation through a family friend at the court of Henry VIII, but his efforts were unsuccessful. To make matters worse, he was terrified to return to his family and admit what he had done. His excessive fear and inability to find help may indicate that the gambling incident was only one in a long list of irresponsible financial and moral choices he had made in recent years. Whatever the explanation, poverty was soon added to his other woes.

Henry Phillips was finally rescued from his predicament by one or more powerful Roman Catholic officials in England. He was given a large amount of money, sent to Louvain in the early months of 1535, and assigned the task of tracking down several English reformers. Even greater rewards were promised to him if he succeeded in his mission. His strategy was to go to Antwerp, posing as a wealthy supporter of religious reform, and establish contacts with the English community.

Foxe's account, which is sometimes very hard to follow, is quite clear in its description of how Phillip's developed a friendship with Tyndale:

*William Tyndale, being in the town of
Antwerp, had been lodged about one whole year
in the house of Thomas Poyntz, an Englishman
who kept there a house of English merchants.
About which time came thither one out of
England, whose name was Henry Philips, his
father being customer of Poole, a comely fellow
like as he had been a gentleman, having a servant
with him, but wherefore he came, or for what purpose he was sent thither, no man could tell.*

*Master Tyndale divers times was desired forth
to dinner and supper amongst merchants; by the
means whereof this Henry Phillips became
acquainted with him, so that within short space
Master Tyndale had a great confidence in him,
and brought him to his lodging to the house of
the said Poyntz; to whom he shewed moreover his
books and other secrets of his study; so little did
Tyndale then mistrust this traitor.*

*But Poyntz having no great confidence in the
fellow, asked Master Tyndale how he came
acquainted with this Phillips. Master Tyndale
answered that he was an honest man, hand-
somely learned and very conformable [i.e.
Lutheran in sympathy]. Then Poyntz, perceiving
that he bare such favour to him, said no more,
thinking that he was brought acquainted with
him by some friend of his.*[1]

Even though Phillips was not recognized as a Roman
Catholic agent, it seems strange that he was able to

establish such a close relationship with Tyndale so rapidly. If Tyndale really understood the danger of his position in Antwerp and was on his guard, how did Phillips earn his trust?

Tyndale's position as an exile provides a partial answer. Like most of those who are forced to leave the place of their birth, he was hungry for news from home. Most of the lands and influence of the Phillips family were in the southwestern counties of Somerset and Dorset, quite close to Tyndale's Gloucestershire roots.

Henry Phillips was also a recent graduate of Oxford, and Tyndale had not been part of a strong academic community for years. It is easy to imagine the wide-ranging discussions they might have had on theology, Bible translation, and even about how life at Oxford had changed since Tyndale's days as a student. With Phillips playing the part of a committed Lutheran, there was no reason for anyone to suspect his real mission.

Yet Thomas Poyntz was suspicious. Phillips asked too many questions and gave too few answers. He was anxious to have Poyntz's help in finding suppliers in Antwerp for a long list of expensive items, but he never seemed to buy anything. He wanted to know all about Poyntz and other businessmen, but seldom gave thorough answers to any of the questions Poyntz asked him in return. Most puzzling of all was the unwillingness of an apparently wealthy man to discuss how he had acquired his money.

Poyntz finally set his doubts aside simply because Tyndale clearly enjoyed and trusted the man. Besides, Thomas Poyntz could not spend all his time looking out for William Tyndale. He had a business to run and was already preparing for a trip to a nearby city that would keep him away from Antwerp for a month or more.

Once Thomas Poyntz left Antwerp, Henry Phillips quickly took steps to earn his reward. Foxe told the story this way:

> In the time of his absence Henry Phillips came again to Antwerp, to the house of Poyntz, and coming in, spake with his wife, asking her for Master Tyndale, and whether he would dine there with him, saying: What good meat shall we have? She answered: Such as the market will give. Then went he forth again, as it is thought, to provide and set the officers which he brought with him from Brussels, in the street and about the door. Then about noon he came again, and went to Master Tyndale, and desired him to lend him forty shillings; for (said he) I lost my purse this morning, coming over at the passage between this and Mechlin. So Master Tyndale took him forty shillings. . . .
>
> Then said Phillips: Master Tyndale, you shall be my guest here this day. No, said Master Tyndale; I go forth this day to dinner, and you shall go with me, and be my guest, where you shall be welcome. So when it was dinner time, Master Tyndale went forth with Phillips and at the going out of Poyntz' house was a long narrow entry, so that two could not go in a front. Master Tyndale would have put Phillips before

170

him, but Phillips would in no wise, but put
Master Tyndale afore, for that he pretended to
shew great humanity. So Master Tyndale, being
a man of no great stature, went before, and
Phillips, a tall comely person, followed behind
him; who had set officers on either side of the
door upon two seats, which, being there, might
see who came in the entry; and coming through
the same entry, Phillips pointed with his finger
over Master Tyndale's head down to him, that
the officers which sat at the door might see that
it was he whom they should take.[2]

Phillips may have been paid by English Roman
Catholics, but when it came time to seize Tyndale he
also relied on help from Charles V, the Holy Roman
Emperor. This gave a facade of legality to the kidnaping.
It's not clear how these officials were able to enter
Antwerp without warning of their arrival being passed
on to the English merchants. They were few in number
and might have hidden both their purpose and identity.
One of them at least must have worked very hard at con-
cealing his identity, however, because as the last part of
Foxe's description makes clear, he was one of the most
powerful men in the emperor's government:

Then they took him, and brought him to the
emperor's attorney or procurer-general, where
he dined. Then came the procurer-general to the
house of Poyntz, and sent away all that was
there of Master Tyndale's, as well his books as

> *other things; and from thence Tyndale was had*
> *to the castle of Vilford, eighteen English miles*
> *from Antwerp, and there he remained until he*
> *was put to death.*[3]

Their plans worked so well that they were able to abduct Tyndale, hold him while he ate with the procurer-general, and remove him from Antwerp without anyone knowing what was happening. It was only when the procurer-general appeared at the English House to seize Tyndale's property that the plot became widely known.

The exact date of Tyndale's abduction is not known, but the best estimates place it on or about May 21, 1535. He was immediately taken to Vilvorde Castle and held there on a charge of heresy.

His place of imprisonment was less than twenty miles from Antwerp, but its proximity to the Roman Catholic strongholds of Brussels and Louvain placed it in a different world, one dedicated to the destruction of independent religious thought.

The castle was an imposing structure, with seven towers, a moat, and three drawbridges. It had been built in 1374 and was patterned after the Bastille in Paris. In Tyndale's day it served as the state prison of the Low Countries. The rising tide of religious violence makes it almost certain that Tyndale was not the only supporter of reform confined within its walls. He was, however, one of the most important.

His capture silenced a gifted translator of the Bible who was also an effective defender of religious reform. It was a clear victory for supporters of the Roman

Catholic Church, especially those who lived in England and had been facing increased pressure from Henry VIII. Tyndale biographer J. F. Mozley summarized both their pleasure and Tyndale's plight with these words: "Within this gloomy stronghold Tyndale would be safe enough, far away from the turbulent and free-thinking city of Antwerp, where the rulers winked at the advance of the Lutheran cause."[4]

Even though Tyndale's kidnaping had been a complete success and the place of his imprisonment was very secure, there were still those who were willing to fight for his release. The English merchants were outraged by the violation of their protected status in Antwerp, and the most furious man among them was Thomas Poyntz. Largely at his urging they wrote letters to Brussels, demanding Tyndale's return, and to London, asking for help from the English government.

Within a few weeks of Tyndale's arrest, word of the situation reached Thomas Cromwell in England. By this time Cromwell was a member of the royal council and a close confidant of Henry VIII, with the title of secretary. He had inherited most of the power formerly wielded by Wolsey, for whom he had previously worked. Cromwell sent Thomas Theobald, his godson and frequent emissary, to Antwerp, Brussels, and Louvain to collect information on the kidnaping. At the end of July 1535, Thomas Theobald submitted a short report to Cromwell and a longer one to Archbishop Thomas Cranmer.

Nearly a month passed without any response from the English government, and Thomas Poyntz grew tired of waiting. He was convinced that strong protests from the business community in Antwerp, English church leaders loyal to Henry VIII, and from the king himself could get Tyndale released. He also feared that there were those close to the king who acted loyal only to maintain a Roman Catholic influence in his government. They would do whatever was necessary to slow or stop any action that might free Tyndale.

On August 25, 1535, Poyntz wrote to his elder brother John, lord of the manor of North Ockendon, northeast of London, in the county of Essex. John had contacts at the court of Henry VIII, and Thomas hoped to use them to put more pressure on the king. "My love of my country," he began, "and my duty to my prince compels me to speak, lest the king be misled and brought into injury by men, yes traitors, who, under colour of forwarding his honour, seek to bring their own purposes to pass. I do not name them, but it is clear that it must be the papists who are at the bottom of it."[5]

Later, Poyntz compared his own motivations to those of the "papists" in England. "But a poor man that has no promotion, nor looks for none, having no quality whereby he might obtain honour, but of a very natural zeal, and fear of God and his prince, had liefer [would gladly] live a beggar all days of his life, and put himself in jeopardy to die, rather than to live and see those leering counsellors to have their purpose."[6]

We do not know how strongly Thomas Poyntz was committed to the cause of religious reform before he met Tyndale, but his friendship with the translator affected him deeply. "Brother," he declared near the end of the letter, "the knowledge that I have of this man causes me to write as my conscience bids me; for the king's grace should have of him at this day as high a treasure as of any one man living."[7]

The letter Thomas Poyntz wrote was forwarded to Cromwell, reaching him by September 21, but Cromwell had already acted. At the end of August 1535, he met with Henry VIII to discuss Tyndale's situation, and by the first week in September two letters were on their way to members of Charles V's government at Brussels. Thomas Poyntz was asked to carry one of these letters and to personally follow up on the responses generated by both of them. Following a very circuitous route, both letters reached their intended recipients sometime between September 10 and 22. By October, Thomas Poyntz was waiting in Brussels for a decision, and it appears he had good reasons for expecting William Tyndale to be released.

Once again, though, he underestimated the malevolent influence of Henry Phillips. Phillips identified Poyntz as a friend of Tyndale and a supporter of Lutheranism and denied that he had any right to present himself as a representative of the English government. Suddenly, Thomas Poyntz found himself under house arrest in Brussels, charged with heresy solely on the evidence presented by Phillips. Over the course of the next three months, Poyntz was examined in detail for religious views contrary to Roman Catholic teachings. Again and again Poyntz engineered delays in the process, hoping to find a way to prove himself innocent and waiting for help from England or Antwerp. By the end of February, he realized that his own life was in danger and that it was only a matter of a few more days before he would be transferred to a much more secure prison. Under cover of darkness, he escaped the relatively light guard kept on him and fled Brussels.

After his flight from imprisonment, Thomas Poyntz was banished from the Netherlands and forced to return to England. He lost most of his possessions in Antwerp, and his business contacts on the Continent were severely disrupted, if not destroyed. Nor was this the only price he paid for trying to rescue Tyndale. His wife, Anna van Calva, who was a native of Antwerp and probably had property or other financial interests there, refused to join him in England and kept his children with her. The debts from his failed business ventures followed Poyntz for years. Not until 1551 was he able to get compensation from the English government for the losses he had suffered. When he died in 1562, his service to God and King Henry VIII was remembered in these words recorded in Latin on his tombstone, "He, for faithful service to his prince and ardent profession of evangelical truth, suffered bonds and imprisonment beyond the sea."[8]

Of all those who tried to save Tyndale, Thomas Poyntz was the only one we know of who was willing to place himself personally at risk. It is one of the greatest ironies of the Protestant Reformation in England that on the tomb of William Tyndale's greatest defender no mention of his name appears.

Perhaps this is not so surprising. On April 13, 1536, Stephen Vaughan wrote again to Cromwell, expressing optimism that Tyndale could still be saved. Strangely, no new attempt was made to free him. Clearly, the final decision in a matter this important was made by King

Henry VIII, but it is not clear why he made it. If he made one attempt to save Tyndale, why let the matter drop, especially after his personal emissary, Thomas Poyntz, had been thrown into prison? Henry was not known for his tolerance toward personal insults and he was well known for his violent retribution against those who interfered with his plans. Even though the English monarch had alienated both the Roman Catholic Church and Charles V, everyone in Europe knew he was a dangerous man. The growing power of the English navy gave him a potent weapon to use against the seaborne commerce of the Holy Roman Empire and Catholic Spain (which Charles also ruled, under the name Charles I).

It is likely that Henry VIII had decided he didn't want William Tyndale released. Henry was obsessed with preserving the political, economic, and social stability of England. He had learned from the chaos unleashed in the German states of the Holy Roman Empire by Luther's teachings that religious stability was the key to achieving that goal.

He had already gained control over most of the power and wealth of the Roman Catholic Church in England. With the help of religious leaders like Cromwell, the king was rapidly transforming it into a national church. To complete that process, Henry VIII needed an English translation of the Bible. He saw Tyndale's translation as the one essential tool needed for establishing a separate religious identity for the English church and ensuring the loyalty of the English people to it.

There was, however, one problem: Henry had no way to guarantee the loyalty of William Tyndale. The example of Martin Luther made it clear just how much trouble a single religious leader could cause. William Tyndale had already shown himself to be a formidable advocate of religious reform, and an independent thinker. He was a man of passionate intensity and quiet dignity who could not be silenced by bribes or intimidation.

If Tyndale was rescued from the hands of Roman Catholic authorities, brought home, and then given the opportunity to finish his work of translation, he would become an English hero. Henry might very well find himself locked in a struggle for control of the English church with a religious celebrity who was both popular and powerful.

He had just been down that road with Sir Thomas More. On July 7, 1535, the former lord chancellor of England had been beheaded because of his refusal to approve the marriage of Henry to Anne Boleyn and to take the oath to the Act of Succession, which involved repudiating the pope's supremacy over the Church of England. His last words were to repeat Psalm Fifty-one and then say, "Pity that should be cut that hath not committed treason."[9] Many in England saw this act as evidence of how merciless their king could be. Even Charles V told the English ambassador, "If I had been master of such a servant, of whose doing I myself have had these many years no small experience, I would rather have lost the best city in my dominions than lose such a worthy councilor."[10]

Still suffering the aftershocks of More's execution by his order, it is not likely that Henry wished to repeat the experience with William Tyndale. It is easy to see how

Henry might have concluded that the famous English translator was a threat to his future plans and needed to be eliminated—but not by him. Who better to do the job than Charles V and the Roman Catholic establishment on the Continent? They were already irreconcilable enemies to both Henry and the new English church.

In the end, Henry did nothing to help William Tyndale. And so another Englishman "suffered bonds and imprisonment beyond the sea" and waited patiently for a destiny he had long expected.

ten

On the day of his arrest, William Tyndale was taken to a meeting with the chief prosecuting attorney for the government of Charles V in the Low Countries. Tyndale had probably never met the procurer-general before, but it is almost certain that he had heard of him.

The man's name was Pierre Dufief, and he was infamous for his ruthlessness and cruelty toward anyone who questioned the authority of the Roman Catholic church. He was passionate about finding and punishing heretics. During interrogations, he often placed great pressure on suspected heretics to give him the information he needed to convict them. Those who did not provide him with the facts he wanted or who did not do so quickly enough were often sent to the torture chamber to restore their clouded memories. One historian of the

Reformation refers to him as "this terrible magistrate."[1]

Once William Tyndale was taken to Vilvorde Castle, the procurer-general visited regularly, bringing a notary with him to make a permanent record of the proceedings. Dufief was interested in many different kinds of information, but his goal was always the same—to collect enough evidence to establish the legal basis, under church law, for a formal charge of heresy.

Dufief would have questioned Tyndale about every aspect of his beliefs, writings, and life in general. This initial process of gathering information might go on for anywhere from a few days to a few months, depending on the complexity of the issues involved and importance of the person being examined. In Tyndale's case, it may have gone on for most of the summer and even into the fall. He had never been one to hold back information about what he believed or what he was doing, so it is unlikely that the rack, the hot iron rod, or any other devices of persuasion were needed to loosen his tongue.

However, Pierre Dufief brought a secret weapon with him. During those early days, Henry Phillips accompanied the procurer-general to the prison but never entered Tyndale's cell. He was still earning his blood money. Phillips was translating Tyndale's writings from English, which few of those involved in the trial understood, into Latin, the official language of both the Roman Catholic Church and the courts.

Pierre Dufief and his helpers were only the first in a long procession of people who examined the English translator. The investigation of William Tyndale was overseen by a commission appointed by a representative of

Charles V. It included four privy councillors from the Holy Roman Empire, three theologians from Louvain, a personal representative of the pope, and various support staff.

At first glance, the commission appeared to be an institution capable of providing an honest evaluation of the heresy charges and conducting a fair trial, if one was necessary. The privy councillors were all lawyers whose task was to act as impartial judges. At least two of the three theologians were well-known and respected scholars. Together they brought to the proceedings a vast knowledge of the Bible and a thorough understanding of church doctrine and practice over the last fifteen hundred years. Their role was not to pass judgement, but to act as expert advisers to the judges on the merits of both the prosecutor's case and defendant's response.

Once the commission was appointed, the procurer-general could not question the prisoner without at least one of the commissioners present. The authority of the commission superceded that of all other courts in the Holy Roman Empire, thus removing it from the influence of local prejudices. The accused was even offered help in preparing his defense. Though the structure necessary for an impartial trial was clearly visible, the commission actually had only two purposes—to prove the guilt of the accused and to impose punishment.

During the investigation of Tyndale, only one of the privy councillors (judges) appears to have taken an active role, and he had far less influence on its outcome than either the theologians or the procurer-general who acted as the prosecutor. All the theologians were anti-Lutheran to the core, and the two best-known scholars were just as notorious as the procurer-general for their excessive zeal in destroying reformers.

James Masson, who was also known as James Latomus or simply Latomus, had demonstrated rare intellectual gifts both as a student and a teacher at Louvain. His extraordinary abilities were narrowly focused on defending the existing structures, practices, and doctrines of the Roman Catholic Church against all attempts at reform.

He was about sixty years old at the time of Tyndale's imprisonment and probably at the height of his intellectual powers. In spite of all his brilliance, he seemed a relic left over from an age long past. Not only was he appalled by Luther's brashly radical ideas, but he also condemned the Christian humanism of Erasmus.

The desire of Erasmus to maintain the most important doctrinal and administrative structures of the Roman Catholic Church, while eliminating corruption, was seen by Latomus as disloyalty to divinely appointed authority. Erasmus insisted that Christian leaders needed to reexamine the biblical basis of their faith. Latomus looked to a particularly impersonal and needlessly complex form of theology developed in the Middle Ages as the ideal guide for orthodox belief and practice.

Erasmus wanted to make the Bible widely available in the common languages of people all over Europe so that they could be taught to apply biblical principles to everyday life. He believed that a renewed emphasis on learning in general and personal piety in particular could revolutionize western civilization and that the influence of the gospel could tame the emerging passion for individual expression.

Latomus saw the wide availability of the Bible as the first step toward doctrinal chaos and social disintegration. He was trying to stop the destruction of Christian civilization as he understood it, but he could not accept that what he was defending was no longer meaningful to most people. His relentless advocacy of the status quo did little to meet the increasingly loud demands from every part of Europe for a more personal understanding of Christianity that emphasized an intimate and passionate relationship with God though Jesus Christ. Mozley is quite correct when he calls Latomus's theology a "grim and merciless intellectualism."[2]

And yet, Latomus was eloquent and knowledgeable. His writing makes him sound very personable. Not surprisingly, he was a hero to many Roman Catholics, and even some of those he attacked admired the man. Erasmus, for example, made favorable comments about the quality and sophistication of his scholarship. Though he was an implacable enemy of reform, Latomus could grab people's attention and compel them to listen. This made him a very dangerous adversary. He could appear reasonable and even kind while arguing for his positions. In the end, he was absolutely committed to destroying those who disagreed with him.

The other prominent theologian who had a part in Tyndale's trial was Ruard Tapper. He was only forty-eight in 1535 and had spent his entire academic life in Louvain. He had earned a doctorate in theology and served as a professor at the school. He was, however, known more for the political power he wielded within the Roman Catholic Church than for his academic achievements. Tapper was chancellor of the university and dean of St. Peter's, the most important church in Louvain. He had been involved in finding and punishing heretics for twelve years.

Tapper was less inclined to scholarly debate than Latomus, even more famous for his zeal, and certainly more cruel in his treatment of those "heretics" he discovered. His attitude toward heresy trials is said to have been summed up by these words: "It is no great matter whether they that die on account of religion be guilty or innocent, provided we terrify the people by such examples; which generally succeeds best, when persons eminent for learning, riches, nobility or high station are thus sacrificed."[3]

With the commission so biased toward proving that William Tyndale was a heretic, it is not surprising that the prosecutor had more power than anyone else to control the outcome of the trial. Pierre Dufief used his position as procurer-general to influence the judges toward a guilty verdict. He also enlisted the help of the theologians, particularly Latomus, in developing and refining his case against the Englishman. His ability to dominate a trial was legendary in the Low Countries, where he had often acted as prosecutor, judge, and executioner in the same case. He clearly enjoyed the fact that no one could question his tactics or authority, since the unique legal status accorded heresy trials placed them outside the jurisdiction of the secular courts.

Dufief was also well paid for his work. He received more than twice as much as anyone else involved in Tyndale's trial. As an added incentive, he was allowed to keep part of the personal property seized for evidence from a suspected heretic, so long as the person was found guilty. The remainder of the prisoner's property was usually sold to pay for the costs of his imprisonment and trial. The level of corruption created by such a system of "justice" is almost impossible to comprehend.

Though the outcome of most heresy trials was a forgone conclusion, it was still important to the Roman Catholic establishment to maintain the appearance of fairness. In order for their eventual victory to be convincing, they had to give William Tyndale a real chance to defend himself. He would have probably been provided with whatever scholarly resources he asked for and been given assistants to help him in preparing his case. He might even have been told that the documents of the trial would be made public, giving him the hope that his defense might reach a larger audience, regardless of the outcome of the trial. What was not said, though Tyndale probably understood it, was that this was almost never done unless the accused recanted his heresy and became a willing ally in the fight against the reformers.

The actual process of arguing back and forth about the correctness or incorrectness of a person's beliefs, especially when a large body of written documents were involved, could go on for months. This exchange of ideas became even more complex if the accused was highly educated. In Tyndale's case, there were other factors that also made his trial longer and more difficult than most.

The guilt or innocence of William Tyndale turned not so much on what he had said or done, but on what he had written. It was therefore critical to have everything written by him available in languages the examiners could understand. This meant that his English works had to be translated into Latin. Apart from the initial examination of Tyndale, the very first task of the procurer-general would have been to create Latin translations of Tyndale's works in English. Henry Phillips was involved in this work probably from the beginning of Tyndale's imprisonment, but clearly there was too much work for one translator to handle in a timely fashion.

In the letter that Thomas Poyntz wrote to his brother asking for the assistance of the English government, he mentioned two Englishmen from Louvain who were translating Tyndale's English works into Latin for use as evidence against him. No one knows if these were in addition to Phillips or if one of them was Phillips, but considering how much had to be translated, it is easy to imagine the task being too large for even three men.

Because Tyndale had chosen to defend himself and was not allowed access to people who shared his views, he needed more time to prepare. He may well have preferred to work alone rather than to accept help from assistants who might sabotage his preparations or at least report everything he was doing to his captors.

Another reason for the length of the trial was created by the arrival of the message from Henry VIII in the fall of 1535. It required a careful response and probably brought work on the trial to a virtual standstill for anywhere from four to six weeks. The situation was further confused by the imprisonment of Thomas Poyntz in November. The procurer-general and at least some of the others who were working on Tyndale's trial would have had to begin examining Poyntz, a personal representative of the king of England. The stakes in this examination were in some ways even higher than those associated with Tyndale because the charges against Poyntz had so much less substance than those against Tyndale.

With all of the delays and difficulties associated with Tyndale's case, it is not likely that a formal list of accusations could have been drawn up by the procurer-general until the end of 1535 or the beginning of 1536.

What was Tyndale doing during this time? Of course he was preparing for his defense, but since the time of his imprisonment, tradition has held that Tyndale continued to work on his translation of the Old Testament and smuggled copies of his work out of his cell.

David Daniell, Tyndale's most recent biographer, is adamant in arguing against this idea. "Whether or not the requests were granted is unknown. The tradition that they were, and that Tyndale spent heroic hours through the long nights of winter in his damp and chilly cell translating Joshua to 2 Chronicles, is pure sentiment. It is also absolutely unlikely. On the one hand, Poyntz did not paint such a picture for Foxe, though he mentioned other manuscripts left behind at Tyndale's death. On the other, the most elementary understanding of the work of translating those books shows that he used a great deal more apparatus than the three books he requested. . . . It is so likely as to be certain that Tyndale would not have had in Vilvorde access to his translator's normal structure of aids; Septuagint, Vulgate, Luther, Jewish commentaries, other published vernacular versions, and a clutch of dictionaries, not to mention friends or employees to act as readers, checkers or scribes."[4]

The idea of Tyndale continuing to work at translating is very compelling, and earlier biographers seemed to think it was possible. Even Daniell cannot make himself utterly abandon the idea. In the midst of his argument that it could not have happened, he inserts a new idea: "Another romance would be harder still to bear—that he had already progressed even beyond Ezra, Nehemiah, and Esther, and was, in those lonely nights of intense suffering, perhaps feeling himself abandoned by his God, now translating the next book, the first extended poetic outburst he would have encountered, the so-appropriate book of Job. What would we not give for Tyndale's Job!"[5] He goes on to discuss the possibility of Tyndale working on the Psalms, Isaiah, and Jeremiah, not so much to produce a usable translation as to keep his hard-won grasp of Hebrew alive.

Whether true or not, the idea of Tyndale continuing with his translation reflects with great accuracy the most important character trait we have seen displayed repeatedly in his life. He was constitutionally incapable of abandoning the dream God had given him. He had been gripped by the need for an English Bible as far back as his days at Little Sodbury Manor, and he had never stopped believing that it could be done or that he was the one to do it. If we know anything about William Tyndale, it is this: if a way could be found to continue with his life's work, he would have found it and used it to his best advantage. Nothing is clearer, nothing is more certain.

By the beginning of October, Tyndale may have been

spending a great deal of time alone in his cell. This would
certainly explain why he was forced to write the letter
requesting warmer clothing in preparation for winter. In
that letter, he also made a very specific request for certain Hebrew study tools:

> *But most of all I beg and beseech your*
> *clemency to be urgent with the commissary, that*
> *he will kindly permit me to have the Hebrew*
> *bible, Hebrew grammar, and Hebrew dictionary,*
> *that I may pass the time in that study. In return*
> *may you obtain what you most desire, so only*
> *that it be for the salvation of your soul. But, to*
> *be carried out before winter, I will be patient,*
> *abiding the will of God, to the glory of the grace*
> *of my Lord Jesus Christ; whose Spirit (I pray)*
> *may ever direct your heart. Amen. W. Tindalus.*[6]

It may be that he asked for these particular items at
this time because they are among the only resources he
had not yet been granted to help him with his defense.
Clearly he would have needed copies of his own works,
Greek and Latin reference materials, and copies of works
by scholars that his prosecutors would refer to. The same
academic resources that Tyndale used to prepare his
defense could also be used to help translate the Old
Testament.

There is also a hint in this section of the letter that
the English scholar may have been mounting a much more
spirited defense than anyone had expected. Could the
words "if any other decision has been taken concerning

me" indicate that he knew his release had been requested? If he did, was he using that knowledge to taunt his captors? Or is it possible that he was using the implied threat presented by Henry VIII's request as a lever to get the Hebrew study material he needed?

All of this is speculation, of course, but Tyndale's passion for the work of translation and his ability to use situations to his advantage makes it unlikely that he would have been idle. Whether he was working on his defense, translating passages from the Bible, or hoping to be released, Tyndale would have been looking for a chance to communicate with the outside world.

Would anyone have been willing or able to help him achieve this goal? Those who were known friends or supporters would have been kept from contacting him. Only those who had exceedingly good Roman Catholic connections would have been able to see this most important prisoner. It is possible that a Roman Catholic refugee from England who had unusually good skills at translating English into Latin might have gotten a job helping Henry Phillips translate Tyndale's works. Henry VIII's government or some group of English reformers at Oxford or Cambridge might have tried to place such a person close to Tyndale in order to communicate with him.

Such an extreme measure, however, may not have been needed to establish contact with the prisoner. A vast network of underground support for reform existed in the Low Countries. A few indications suggest that these people even worked in the government of Charles V. It seems more than likely that Tyndale was able to get some material out and some messages were able to reach him through a highly placed Roman Catholic official with secret reform sympathies.

This leads inevitably to the question, If Tyndale was able to smuggle material out, where is it? Why wasn't it used for propaganda purposes after his death? It would have been very valuable to the reformers for use in enhancing the image of one of their most important martyrs. Even the Roman Catholic Church might have used the records of Tyndale's defense to show how their theologians had defeated him. Why in all the years since his imprisonment hasn't anything other than a single letter from prison come to light?

Mozley points to a passage from Foxe which gives a place to begin constructing an answer. On the morning of Tyndale's death, wrote Foxe, "He delivered a letter to the keeper of the castle; which the keeper himself brought to the house of the aforesaid Poyntz in Antwerp shortly after; which letter with his examinations [before the commissioners] and other his disputations [with Louvain] I would might have come to our hands: all of which, I understand, did remain, and yet perhaps do, in the hands or the keeper's daughter."[7]

Here is clear evidence of documents that were passed on to someone after Tyndale's death. Besides the letter to the Poyntz family, these papers apparently included a record of Tyndale's defense against the charges of heresy and were all given to the family of the man who managed Vilvorde Castle.

Why couldn't Foxe get his hands on them and why has no trace of them appeared? They may have been taken from the keeper by Roman Catholic officials and then hidden or destroyed. They may have been sent back to England through the reform underground, eventually reaching Henry VIII. The king may have hidden them to reduce the stature of Tyndale and give greater weight to the idea of an "authorized version" of the English Bible, released by authority of the king.

There is no way to tell what may have happened to such documents, but to maintain that they were never created and had no way to escape the imprisonment that held Tyndale does not fit what is known either of the man or of the records that do exist.

It is important to remember that Tyndale's letter requesting the Hebrew study tools was buried for hundreds of years in the government archives at Brussels, the last place anyone might have thought to look. Other documents may still be waiting to be found in musty government archives or in the little-used storage facilities of a dozen different universities in Europe.

Once the official charges against Tyndale were presented in early 1536, it was time to put his preparation to the test. Written exchanges between himself and his accusers continued for months. They covered familiar territory—salvation by faith alone; supremacy of the pope; the nature of communion. Both sides treated each other with respect. Tyndale's accusers would have wanted to give him every reason to recant, for having such a respected scholar turn away from reformation ideals would have been the greatest victory they could gain. Tyndale would have had hopes of convincing at least one of these men to look at God's Word with fresh eyes.

At the heart of the debate was a simple question, What does the Bible say? For the first time in more than one thousand years, a majority of the people in Europe had the opportunity to read the Bible and decide for themselves. They knew that the power to make this decision had come to them because of the hard work and sacrifices of men like Erasmus, Luther, and Tyndale. They were deeply grateful and tremendously excited.

Those who spent time with Tyndale during his imprisonment were not simply moved by his scholarly achievements. They were struck by his courage, conviction, and decency. He had not only translated the Bible into English, but he had transplanted its principles into his daily life, and the message of his character was displayed in a language that needed no translator to make it clear.

Foxe recorded these details about the impact of his life: "Such was the power of his doctrine and the sincerity of his life, that during the time of his imprisonment, which endured a year and a half, he converted his keeper, the keeper's daughter, and others of his household. Also the rest that were with Tyndale conversant in the castle, reported of him, that if he were not a good Christian man, they could not tell whom they might take to be one."[8]

Another indication of his influence given by Foxe seems almost too incredible to be true, were it not confirmed by Edward Hall, the sixteenth-century English historian. These are Halls words: "But yet this report did the Procurator general there (which we call here the Lieutenant) make of him, that he was, *homo doctus, pius et bonus,* that is to say, learned, godly, and good."[9] Even the corrupt and jaded Pierre Dufief could not escape the impact of Tyndale's character.

That William Tyndale could elicit such a response from someone who was trying to destroy him leads to one further conclusion. If he had not had opportunities to get written material out of prison earlier, it is almost certain that, as the trial neared its end, more people would have begun to see Tyndale as a victim of Roman Catholic brutality and want to help him communicate with Lutheran sympathizers outside the prison walls.

But all the goodwill in the world could not save him from the ruthlessly efficient machinery of the heresy trial. In early August 1536, Tyndale was condemned as a heretic and sentenced to be degraded (removed from the priesthood) and executed. Now was the time for those who had worked so long to capture and convict William Tyndale to declare victory in a public ceremony held in the town that had grown up around Vilvorde Castle and shared its name. It was a lavish event. All the members of the commission which had conducted Tyndale's trial were probably there. One or more dignitaries would act as personal representatives of the pope. Three Roman Catholic bishops shared the responsibilities for conducting the service. The procurer-general had an important part to play in the ceremonies.

Representatives from Louvain were probably on hand to share in the victory achieved by Latomus, Tapper, and other members of their academic community. Influential officials from Brussels would have attended to show their support of Charles V and the Holy Roman Empire. Local government and business leaders from many smaller communities all around Vilvorde would likely have attended to show their support as well. No one from Antwerp is mentioned as having attended.

It is not certain where the event was held. A public square would be the most likely place, but churches were sometimes used for this purpose as well. In either case, the three bishops sat on a raised platform where they were easily visible. William Tyndale was brought to them, dressed in the vestments of the priesthood. He was forced to kneel before them. The specific charges of heresy were read aloud, and he was declared guilty. His hands were carefully scraped with a knife or some other object as the symbolic removal of the anointing oil he had received at the time of his ordination. The bread and wine of communion were placed in his hands and then taken away. His priestly clothing was removed one piece at a time, and he was then dressed as a layperson.

During the process, ominous pronouncements continued to be made about his unworthiness to be a priest and his separation from the community of faith. After he had been degraded from the priesthood, the presiding bishop handed him over to Pierre Dufief, the official representative of the secular government.

With pro-reform sentiments so widely held, even in Roman Catholic circles, the thought must have passed through more than one mind that the bishops and other religious play-actors performing this ritual were the ones truly degraded by it.

If normal procedure had been followed, William Tyndale would have died a few days after his removal from the priesthood. Instead, approximately two months passed.

It is possible that some members of the commission who had not been directly involved in questioning the prisoner were uncomfortable passing sentence on so prominent a reformer without the official authorization of Charles V. The emperor was fighting a war in southeast France, and it would have taken a couple weeks before a message could be sent to him and returned. It is even possible that some final plea for leniency was heard from England, Antwerp, or one of the German states.

The time was not wasted. A final attempt was made to get Tyndale to recant, which would have provided an even greater victory than killing him. Mozley's description of the process makes it sound quite unpleasant. "Relays of priests and monks would be sent to work upon the weakness or weariness of a condemned man. It was vain for the victim to beg to be left in peace, or to plead that his mind was fully settled; the unwelcome visitors were ruthless in their attentions."[10]

There is not the slightest indication that these final efforts moved Tyndale at all. He had dedicated most of his life to these kinds of battles. In his last letter to John Frith, written in the summer of 1531 just before the young Englishman was burned at the stake, the translator had offered his friend this advice: "Fear not men that threat, nor trust men that speak fair: but trust him that is true of promise, and able to make his word good. Your cause is Christ's gospel, a light that must be fed with the blood of faith. The lamp must be dressed and snuffed daily, and that oil poured in every evening and morning, that the light go not out."[11]

William Tyndale, who had already done so much to

give the world the light of the gospel, did not waiver when the time came to perform his final task.The end came in the early days of October 1536. Foxe's account is very short, as if death were a small thing when measured against Tyndale's accomplishments and his hope for the future. "At last, after much reasoning, when no reason would serve, although he deserved no death, he condemned by virtue of the emperor's decree. . .and, upon the same, brought forth to the place of execution, was there tied to the stake, and then strangled first by the hangman, and afterwards with fire consumed, in the morning at the town of Vilvorde, A.D. 1536: crying thus at the stake with a fervent zeal, and a loud voice, 'Lord! open the king of England's eyes.' "[12]

From other accounts of such executions, we can construct a bit more detailed picture of Tyndale's last moments. The execution was carried out in public, perhaps at the same spot where the bishops had previously removed Tyndale from the priesthood. Efforts were made to assemble as large a crowd as possible on the day appointed for the punishment of the heretic.

The prisoner was lead through the crowd until he reached a barricade surrounding a large, circular area. In the middle of the circle, a cross made of two large timbers was set upright in the ground, standing perhaps six or seven feet high. At the top, iron chains were fastened. A noose, made from hemp rope, was also hanging loosely from the top of the upright timber, with the ends of the rope passing back through holes in the beam. The procurer-general and the commission that had convicted Tyndale were sitting off to one side of the circle.

The prisoner was led through the barricade, accompanied by his guards and the executioner. One last time, he was asked to recant his heresies. If he did not, he was taken to the cross and given a short time to pray. Then his feet were securely attached to the bottom of the post. The upper chain was secured around his neck, and the noose was placed around his neck. Next, brushwood, straw and logs were packed around the condemned man, forming a small hut around him. A sprinkling of gunpowder was added to make the fire burn hotter.

The executioner moved to stand behind the cross and picked up the ends of noose, removing most of the slack. At a signal from the procurer-general, he jerked the noose tight, strangling his victim. The procurer-general watched the prisoner die. When he was sure all signs of life had ceased, he took a lighted torch of wax and handed it to the executioner who set the wooden structure on fire.

Tyndale's last prayer was answered within one year of his death, when Henry VIII granted licenses to Matthew's and Coverdale's Bibles. Within two years, Thomas Cromwell, acting for the king, ordered that every parish church in England make a copy of the Great Bible available for public reading.

William Tyndale's English ploughman would have the Word of God at last.

epilogue

William Tyndale's life ended, but his legacy continued. In fact, it can still be felt today.

The first two Bibles authorized by King Henry VIII were the Matthew's Bible and the Coverdale Bible. Both contained an almost verbatim copy of Tyndale's New Testament and relied heavily on his translations of the Pentateuch and other parts of the Old Testament. The Matthew's Bible was edited by John Rogers, who had been chaplain at the English House in Antwerp when Tyndale lived there. The Coverdale Bible was produced by Miles Coverdale, whom Tyndale had also known.

Coverdale later edited the Great Bible which also draws heavily from Tyndale's work. (It gets its name from its large size.) In 1537, King Henry ordered a copy of the Great Bible to be chained in every church. Within two years, complaints were pouring in about the crowds of people standing around the Bible during services and reading the words so loudly that it was disrupting church. In response, Henry ordered that people refrain from reading the Bible during services.

The appearance of an English Bible helped spark a rapid rise in literacy among the English people. Tyndale was without a doubt the most significant contributor to the English language between Chaucer and Shakespeare. In a real sense William Tyndale made Shakespeare possible by presenting him with a rapidly developing language ready for poetic experimentation and by helping create a literate population eager to attend his plays and buy printed copies of them. Words still used today, such as *Jehovah, mercy seat, Passover,* and *scapegoat* were first coined by Tyndale. "With God all things are possible," "Be not weary in well doing," and "Behold, I stand at the door and knock," are phrases first written five hundred years ago when William Tyndale translated the New Testament into English.

Tyndale's influence on Bible translation continued when the King James Version appeared at the beginning of the seventeenth century. More than eighty percent of the New Testament was taken directly from Tyndale's work, and a similar dependence on his skills as a translator is apparent in those parts of the Old Testament that he had completed.

Through the King James Version, William Tyndale has continued to shape the culture of the English speaking world, even to our day. Only the second half of the twentieth century has seen a greater emphasis on translating the Bible than did his own century, a century in which he was the central, though unacknowledged, English translator. During the late 1900s, the King James Version, with its huge reliance on Tyndale's skills, was constantly held up as the unequaled model for pure literary power that other translators strove to emulate.

William Tyndale's mission to give the English ploughman a Bible has been carried on by other translators throughout the world who continue to translate God's Word into languages that never before have appeared in writing. This, perhaps, would be the legacy of which William Tyndale would be most pleased.

Notes

Introduction
1. J. F. Mozley, *William Tyndale* (1937, reprint, Westport, Conn.: Greenwood Press, 1971), p. 334.
2. Ibid.

Chapter 1
1. Augustine, "On the Work of Monks," trans. H. Browne, in *St Augustin: On the Holy Trinity, Doctrinal Treatises, Moral Treatises,* Philip Schaff, ed., vol. 3 in A Select Library of the Nicene and Post-Nicene Fathers of the Christian Church (1887, reprint, Grand Rapids, Mich.: Eerdmans, 1978), p. 521.
2. Brian Edwards, *William Tyndale: The Father of the English Bible* (Farmington Hills, Mich.: William Tyndale College, 1982), p. 44.

Chapter 2
1. Philip Schaff, *The Middle Ages (Part II): A.D. 1294–1517,* vol. 6 of History of the Christian Church (1910, reprint, Grand Rapids, Mich.: Eerdmans, 1970), p. 647.
2. Will Durant, *The Reformation: A History of European Civilization from Wyclif to Calvin: 1300–1564,* vol. 6 of The Story of Civilization (New York: Simon & Schuster, 1957), p. 523.
3. Ibid., p. 285.

Chapter 3
1. Durant, p. 528.
2. Durant, p. 531.
3. John Foxe, *Acts and Monuments.* 1563, pp. 513–14,

quoted in David Daniell, *William Tyndale: A Biography* (New Haven, Conn.: Yale, 1994), p. 62.

4. Edwards, p. 56.

5. "W. T. to the Reader" in *Tyndale's Old Testament: Being the Pentateuch of 1530, Joshua to 2 Chronicles of 1537, and Jonah.* trans. by William Tyndale, ed. by David Daniell (New Haven, Conn.: Yale, 1992), p. 4.

6. Foxe, vol. 5, pp. 116–17, quoted in Daniell, p. 77.

7. Tyndale, *Tyndale's Old Testament,* p. 4.

8. Daniell, p. 78.

9. F. Douglas Price, "Gloucester Diocese under Bishop Hooper, 1551–3." *Translations of the Bristol and Gloucestershire Archaelogical Society,* LX, 1938, pp. 51–151, quoted in Daniels, p. 78.

10. Edwards, p. 61.

Chapter 4

1. Edwards, p. 65.

2. Tyndale, *Tyndale's Old Testament,* p. 5.

3. Ibid.

4. Ibid.

5. S. Harrison Thompson, *Europe in Renaissance and Reformation* (New York: Harcourt, Brace & World, 1963), p. 485.

6. Ibid., p. 485.

7. Edwards, pp. 75–76.

8. Thompson, pp. 485–86.

9. Edwards, pp. 77–78.

10. Daniell, p. 103.

11. Tyndale, *Tyndale's Old Testament,* p. 5.

12. Daniell, p. 102.

Chapter 5

1. Durant, pp. 383–84.
2. Ibid., p. 386.
3. Ibid., p. 390.
4. Ibid., p. 392.
5. Ibid., p. 393.
6. Ibid., p. 349.
7. Edwards, p. 81.
8. Ibid., p. 81.
9. William Tyndale, *Tyndale's New Testament*, ed. David Daniell (New Haven: Yale, 1995), pp. 361–62.
10. Tyndale, *New Testament*, p. 362.
11. Daniell, pp. 112–13.
12. Tyndale, *New Testament*, p. 161.
13. Mozley, p. 56.
14. Daniell, p. 109.

Chapter 6

1. Mozley, pp. 59–60.
2. Edwards, p. 88.
3. Daniell, p. 146.
4. Ibid., p. 134.
5. Edwards, p. 89.
6. F. C. Avis, "Book Smuggling into England during the Sixteenth Century," *Gutenberg Jarhbuch,* 1972, p. 184, quoted in Daniell, p. 186.
7. L. A. Schuster, "Thomas More's Polemical Career, 1523–1533," in *CWM,* VIII, iii, pp. 1135–267, quoted in Daniell, p. 187.
8. Edwards, p. 92.
9. Ibid., p. 93.

10. Daniell, p. 194.
11. Edwards, p. 93.
12. Daniell, p. 175.
13. Ibid., p. 143.
14. Ibid., p. 143.

Chapter 7

1. Foxe, vol. 4, p. 621, quoted in Daniell, p. 176.
2. Daniell, p. 177.
3. Ibid., p. 195.
4. Mozley, p. 122.
5. Daniell, pp. 168–69.
6. Edwards, p. 108.
7. Ibid., p. 108.
8. Mozley, p. 129.
9. Edwards, p. 125.
10. Tyndale, *Tyndale's Old Testament,* p. 114.
11. Tyndale, *Tyndale's Old Testament,* p. 234.
12. Edwards, p. 115.
13. Daniell, p. 201.
14. Ibid., p. 202.

Chapter 8

1. Daniell, p. 210.
2. Ibid., pp. 213–14.
3. Ibid., p. 270.
4. Ibid., p. 216.
5. Ibid., pp. 184–85.
6. Ibid., p. 219.
7. Ibid.
8. Mozley, pp. 251–52.
9. Ibid., pp. 254–55.

10. Edwards, pp. 129–30.
11. Durant, p. 546.
12. Daniell, p. 324.
13. Tyndale, *Tyndale's New Testament,* pp. 13–14.
14. Daniell, p. 330.

Chapter 9
1. Mozley, p. 294.
2. Ibid., p. 296.
3. Ibid., p. 297.
4. Ibid., p. 302.
5. Ibid., p. 309.
6. Ibid., p. 310.
7. Ibid., p. 311.
8. Ibid., p. 319.
9. Durant, p. 558.
10. Ibid., p. 558.

Chapter 10
1. Mosley, p. 326.
2. Ibid., p. 325.
3. Ibid., p. 326.
4. Daniell, p. 380.
5. Ibid.
6. Mozley, pp. 334–5.
7. Ibid., pp. 340–341.
8. Ibid., p. 337.
9. Daniell, p. 381.
10. Mozley, p. 340.
11. Ibid., p. 257.
12. Ibid., p. 341.

HEROES OF THE FAITH

This exciting biographical series explores the lives of famous Christian men and women throughout the ages. These trade paper books will inspire and encourage you to follow the example of these "Heroes of the Faith" who made Christ the center of their existence. 208 pages each. Only $3.97 each!

Gladys Aylward, Missionary to China
Sam Wellman

Brother Andrew, God's Undercover Agent
Alan Millwright

Corrie ten Boom, Heroine of Haarlem
Sam Wellman

*William and Catherine Booth,
Founders of the Salvation Army*
Helen Hosier

*John Bunyan,
Author of* The Pilgrim's Progress
Sam Wellman

William Carey, Father of Missions
Sam Wellman

Amy Carmichael, Abandoned to God
Sam Wellman

Fanny Crosby, the Hymn Writer
Bernard Ruffin

Jonathan Edwards, The Great Awakener
Helen Hosier

Jim Elliot, Missionary to Ecuador
Susan Miller

Charles Finney, The Great Revivalist
Bonnie Harvey

Billy Graham, the Great Evangelist
Sam Wellman

C.S. Lewis, Author of Mere Christianity
Sam Wellman

Martin Luther, the Great Reformer
Dan Harmon

George Müller, Man of Faith
Bonnie Harvey

*David Livingstone,
Missionary and Explorer*
Sam Wellman

*George Washington Carver,
Inventor and Naturalist*
Sam Wellman

*D. L. Moody,
the American Evangelist*
Bonnie Harvey

*Samuel Morris,
the Apostle of Simple Faith*
W. Terry Whalin

*Mother Teresa,
Missionary of Charity*
Sam Wellman

Watchman Nee, Man of Suffering
Bob Laurent

John Newton, Author of "Amazing Grace"
Anne Sandberg

Florence Nightingale, Lady with the Lamp
Sam Wellman

Mary Slessor, Queen of Calabar
Sam Wellman

Charles Spurgeon, the Great Orator
Dan Harmon

*Hudson Taylor, Founder,
China Inland Mission*
Vance Christie

Sojourner Truth, American Abolitionist
W. Terry Whalin

John Wesley, the Great Methodist
Sam Wellman

Available wherever books are sold.
Or order from:
Barbour Publishing, Inc.
P.O. Box 719
Uhrichsville, Ohio 44683
http://www.barbourbooks.com

If you order by mail, add $2.00 to your order for shipping.
Prices subject to change without notice.